INSIGHT

CORK &
SOUTHWEST
IRELAND

before

Discovery
CHANNEL

APA PUBLICATIONS
Part of the Langenscheidt Publishing Group

L

Ireland

65 km / 40 miles

ATLANTIC OCEAN

NORTHERN IRELAND

IRELAND (EIRE)

Islay
KINTYRE
Arran
Campbeltown

North Channel

Ballycastle
Buncrana
Coleraine
LONDONDERRY
Ballymoney
Larne
Letterkenny (Leitir Ceanainn)
Maghera
Ballymena
Strabane
Antrim
Bangor
Donegal
Cookstown
Dungannon
Lough Neagh
BELFAST
Lisburn
Omagh
Ballyshannon
Enniskillen
Monaghan (Muineachán)
Armagh
Downpatrick
Sligo (Sligeach)
Cuilcagh 665
Cavan (An Cabhán)
Newry
Ballina (Béal an Átha)
Castlebar (Caislean an Bharraigh)
Carrick-on-Shannon
Dunleer
DUNDALK (Dún Dealgan)
Irish Sea
Nephin 804
Castlerea
Kells (Ceanannus Mór)
DROGHEDA (Droichead Átha)
Castlebar
Westport
Claremorris
Roscommon
Longford (An Longfort)
Navan (An Uaimh)
Skerries
Swords (Sord)
Ballinrobe
Tuam (Tuaim)
Athlone (Baile Átha Luain)
Mullingar (An Muileann gCearr)
DUBLIN (Baile Átha Cliath)
Ballinasloe (Béal Átha na Sluaighe)
Tullamore (Tulach Mhór)
Dún Laoghaire
GALWAY (Gaillimh)
Loughrea
Birr
Naas (An Nás)
Bray (Bré)
Portarlington
Kildare
Wicklow (Cill Mhantáin)
Roscrea (Ros Cré)
Portlaoise (Port Laoise)
Ennistymon
Carlow (Ceatharlach)
Arklow (An tinbhear Mór)
Ennis (Inis)
Nenagh (An tAonach)
Castlecomer
Gorey
Kilrush
Thurles (Durlas)
Kilkenny (Cill Chainnigh)
LIMERICK (Luimneach)
Cashel (Caiseal)
Enniscorthy (Inis Córthaidh)
Listowel
Newcastle West
Tipperary
Clonmel (Cluain Meala)
Wexford (Loch Garman)
Tralee (Trá Lí)
Rath Luirc
Cahir (An Chathair)
New Ross (Ros Mhic Thriúin)
Brandon Mtn 951
Mitchelstown
Knockmealdown 793
WATERFORD (Port Láirge)
Baurtregaum 850
Castleisland
Mallow (Mala)
Fermoy
Dungarvan (Dún Garbhán)
St George's Channel
Killorglin
Carrantuohill 1041
Mangerton Mtn 838
Macroom
KILLARNEY (Cill Áirne)
CORK (Corcaigh)
Youghal (Eochaill)
Cahirciveen
Ballincollig
Cobh (An Cóbn)
Bantry
Kinsale
Clonakilty
Skibbereen

Celtic Sea

Welcome!

This is one of 133 itinerary-based Pocket Guides produced by the editors of Insight Guides, whose books have set the standard for visual travel guides since 1970. With top-quality photography and authoritative recommendations, this guidebook brings you the very best of the region in a series of 17 tailor-made routes.

Rachel Warren, Insight's correspondent in southwest Ireland, helps visitors to get the most out of this region's many attractions, from rainbow-coloured market towns to picturesque fishing villages and lakes to low hills dotted with stone circles, to abbeys and castles. The itineraries begin in Cork city, move on to west Cork, then up to Bantry Bay and the Beara Peninsula, Killarney and the Ring of Kerry and then to the Dingle Peninsula. Supporting the itineraries are sections on history and culture, eating out, nightlife and festivals plus a chapter on useful practical information, including a list of hand-picked hotels in a range of prices.

 Rachel Warren was born in London to Irish parents, and spent most of her childhood holidays on her uncle's farm near Clonakilty. After working in London as a journalist specialising in travel and food, while renovating a stone cottage 'halfway up a west Cork mountain', she decided to become a freelance author based in Kinsale. She says of her adopted home, 'I still get excited about exploring the southwest, and like nothing better than showing friends around, and making new discoveries. Once they've got over the amazing scenery and the slower pace of life, what most impresses my visitors is the genuine friendliness they meet at every turn – especially in pubs. I've probably learnt more about the southwest over the years from pubs than I have from books and museums.'

C O N T E N T S

Pages 2/3:
Ballinskelligs
Bay

Cork and Kerry have always stood apart from the rest of Ireland. Their location, deep in the southwest of the country, makes them the two furthest counties from the capital, Dublin, and hence the least subject to the city's influence. Kerry has such an independent attitude of mind that its nickname is The Kingdom, as if it even had its own laws, while Cork is known as the Rebel County. While the eastern seaboard of Ireland had close ties with England and Wales, up until the 18th century Cork and Kerry maintained trading links with France and Spain.

Stronghold Mountains

Even today the hilly, so-called mountainous parts of Cork and Kerry can feel quite uncannily remote. It is possible to drive for 10, even 20 miles without seeing a sign of human habitation.

The very first settlers arrived by sea from mainland Europe, primarily Spain, around 6000BC. By 2000BC they had been joined by various waves of Celtic settlers. These are the people who built the stone circles, wedge tombs and cooking pits that dot the hills of Cork and Kerry. Not much is known about them, but it is apparent that they had a good grasp of astronomy, as all their circles are built to face either the summer or the winter solstice.

Ardgroom Stone Circle

Christianity was brought to Ireland, according to the official version, in AD432 by Saint Patrick. Many archaeologists claim that there is evidence of Christian settlements in isolated spots, like the Old Head of Kinsale and the Skellig Rocks, 100 years earlier.

There followed a period which has been much idealised, in which Christianity and the Celtic world survived in relative harmony. Old Irish society was Celtic, based on a strict hierarchical world order in which wealth was calculated in terms of cattle. The warlords lived within earth-walled ring forts, known in Irish as *dúns, raths* or *líos*. The earth walls were topped by palisades, and whenever there was fear of a raid all the cattle were herded into the fort. These earth forts, and the earlier stone circles, have survived to this day, chiefly due to superstitions which stopped the farmers from interfering with them, as they were believed to be 'fairy forts'.

At around the same time, Irish monasticism was flourishing. The most important religious centre in the southwest was founded by St

Staigue Ring Fort

Finbar at Gougane Barra, a beautiful deep tarn in the west Cork hills. The Skellig Rocks were occupied by another monastic foundation; Rosscarbery had its university; St Kieran ministered to the people of Cape Clear island; and St Brendan set sail for America from the Dingle shore. Schull received its name from its *scoil* or school for the religious.

These early monks had a brilliant knack of choosing the most beautiful places in which to set up their communities. In the 7th century, a monastic brotherhood settled on Innisfallen Island in the midst of Killarney's lakes, little knowing that the spot chosen for its peaceful isolation would become a magnet for visitors from all over the world.

The European Invasion

Ireland's position off the extreme west of the European mainland made it one of the few places in Europe never to be conquered by the Romans. This is one of the reasons why Irish culture retained its identity for so long, and why even today Ireland is distinctly different from the rest of the Continent.

The first hostile European invaders were the Vikings, who did not make much of an impression on the southwest, preferring to make their mark on the southeast coast instead. The Anglo-Normans arrived in 1169. However, they quickly intermarried with the native families and became, in the words of the chronicler Geraldus of Wales, 'more Irish than the Irish'.

Blarney Castle

It was during the next two centuries that much of Ireland's ecclesiastical architecture originated. Norman influence also led to the abandoning of earth forts and a great concentration of stone castle-building. Blarney is the best surviving example of these castles, which were, in effect, fortified tower houses. More than 400 were built in Cork county alone.

The Flight of the Earls

Ireland was nominally ruled from England, although life went on for the Irish clan chiefs much as it always had. Trouble started when England's Queen Elizabeth I, following disputes with Rome, adopted the reformed church as the official religion, and expected her subjects, including the Irish, to do the same. In 1598, the Irish chieftains began to organise against the order to abandon their religion. The Spanish landed at Kinsale in 1601 to support the Irish Catholics against the English. However, the combined Irish and Spanish forces were resoundingly defeated at the Battle of Kinsale, and the clan chiefs left Ireland for Spain in a movement known as 'The Flight of the Earls'. One of the Earls, Donal Cam O'Sullivan Beare, retreated to his castle at Dunboy near Castletownbere after the defeat at Kinsale. Dunboy remained untaken for six months, and eventually its heroic and greatly outnumbered defenders were killed when they blew it up rather than surrender. O'Sullivan himself escaped to Ulster, and died in exile in Spain.

The English Plantation

Repression of the Catholic religion continued throughout the 16th and 17th centuries. Most of the ruined ecclesiastical buildings located around Cork and Kerry were sacked and abandoned during these troubled years.

In order to ensure the loyalty of their Irish subjects, the English used a method known as 'plantation'. This consisted of granting lands that had been confiscated from Irish clan chiefs to Englishmen, often ex-soldiers, who could be counted on to remain loyal to the Crown and to the reformed religion. A wall plaque in Castletownshend's church gives a vivid history of three such families, who intermarried, built big houses and generally prospered, while remaining, some of them to this very day, apparently quite English in accent, manners and religious observance.

Not surprisingly, the presence of these newcomers, often living on land confiscated from

William of Orange

relatives of their impoverished Irish neighbours, was often resented. During the troubles of the 1920s, many of these so-called 'Big Houses' were burnt to the ground by nationalist forces in an understandable, but nevertheless, spiteful act of revenge.

Penal but Prosperous Years

In 1691, William of Orange landed in Ireland and defeated the Jacobite forces at Aughrim. The Treaty of Limerick ended a century of warfare. The new Irish Parliament was dominated by Protestants, who passed a number of 'Penal Laws'. These forbade Catholics to practise their religion, to buy land, hold commissions in the army, enter the liberal professions, or even to own a horse worth more than £5.

The further from Dublin, the less strictly enforced these laws were, and in Cork and Kerry, the 18th century was a time of relative prosperity. Cork was an important butter-exporting centre. The butter was carried to the city from its rural hinterland on small tracks known as 'butter roads'. Many of these have now been incorporated into walking routes. The 18th century also saw much house building in a nicely proportioned classical style.

Irish kitchen in the 1840s

Meanwhile the population was growing rapidly. Competition for land was intense, and rents went ever higher. Methods of agriculture, and rural life in general, remained primitive. The only change from 100 years earlier was the increased reliance for sustenance, particularly of the poorest people, on the potato, which was introduced to Ireland in the 1500s on ships returning from South America.

The Liberator

Increased national awareness and the spread of French Revolutionary ideas were among the factors that led to the Society of United Irishmen in 1791. One of their leaders, Wolfe Tone, sought help from France, and returned to Bantry Bay in 1796 at the head of an invading fleet, only to be prevented from landing by bad weather.

In the end, it was not armed rebellion that regained the civil rights of the Catholic population, but the powers of oratory and the organisation of a lawyer from Kerry, Daniel O'Connell (1775–1847). Also known as 'The Liberator', O'Connell orchestrated a massive display of support through large public meetings, and in 1829 the Catholic Emancipation Bill was passed. This removed the oath on entering Parliament, which no Catholic had been able to swear, replacing it with a generally acceptable oath of allegiance. O'Connell himself was among those Catholic MPs now able to take their seats at Westminster in London.

Famine and Emigration

The failure of the potato crop between 1845 and 1850 led to widespread famine. The coastal areas of west Cork and the Dingle peninsula, which then, as now, consisted largely of small subsistence farms, were especially badly hit. It is hard to imagine as you drive through today how anyone could starve to death with such fertile land and richly stocked seas. But this is to forget the scale of the famine. So many people were competing for what little food was available that it is said there was not a scrap of seaweed left on the shore between Baltimore and Schull. Some of the older generation still refuse to eat mussels, dismissing them as 'famine food'.

The Beara and the Iveragh peninsulas lost three-quarters of their populations in the 10 years between 1845 and 1855. The population of Ireland as a whole dropped from 8.5 million in 1845 to 6.5 million in 1851. A million died from hunger or disease and

even more emigrated, either to mainland Britain or to the New World. Many of those who reached North America carried with them an enduring hatred of what they saw as Britain's indifference to their fate, and a number of them became radical in their political outlook, founding both the Irish Republican Brotherhood and the Fenian organisation, which sought independence from British rule, by violent means if necessary.

Independence and Beyond

The question of Home Rule and ownership of the land dominated the rest of the 19th century and various organisations were formed to resist the 'alien aristocracy'. Eventually, in 1916, while England was preoccupied with the war in Europe, a small band of Irish Volunteers staged the Easter Rising in

Irish emigrants

Dublin. Although the revolt lacked widespread popular support and was put down within a week by British forces, the subsequent ruthless execution of its leaders by the British authorities turned the tide of sentiment in favour of the rebels. Between then and 1921, Britain and Ireland were effectively at war, with the Irish Republican Army pitted against British police and troops. Much of the fighting took the form of guerrilla warfare, with small 'flying columns' wreaking havoc. There was much activity among the mountains of west Cork and in the streets of Cork city.

Children celebrating the end of the Anglo-Irish war

A treaty was signed in 1921, but its terms sparked a civil war which divided the country in 1922–23 over the issue of whether the new Irish Government should allow six counties of Ulster to remain part of the United Kingdom, or hold out for a united Ireland. Michael Collins, the chief of staff of the new Irish Army, was a prominent victim of the conflict. Pragmatically, he favoured the compromise treaty dividing the island, and was shot by the opposing faction in an ambush outside Macroom, near his birthplace in Clonakilty.

The Southwest Today

The problem of a divided Ireland has not gone away, but these days violence is only a distant memory in the southwest. Rather than looking inward, once again the region looks to Europe, this time to the European Union which provides lifeline subsidies for many of the area's small farmers and fishermen.

Since joining the EC, now the EU, in 1973, rural Ireland has made a leap from the 19th into the 21st century. While rural electrification was complete by the mid-1950s, many small farmers preferred to do things the old way. Much of the equipment now seen in 'agricultural museums' was still in use on the farm less than 30 years ago.

European funds have been used to upgrade the southwest's main roads, and to improve hotels and other accommodation. Where once a feature of a holiday in the area was that there was virtually nothing to do in the cultural tourism line apart from walk around a few unlabelled ruins, nowadays a sudden rash of interpretative centres has sprung up, of varying degrees of usefulness.

While there is a certain amount of high-tech light industry (chemicals, computer components) in the southwest, agriculture and tourism remain the chief sources of income. Because this has traditionally been a farming area, the unhurried rural way of life and the pristine beauty of the countryside have survived to such an extent that many visitors feel they are stepping backwards into a kind of time-warp.

Race to the top

Several hundred outsiders, or 'blow-ins' as they are called locally – some from the US, but mainly Irish and European – have settled in the more scenic parts of Cork and Kerry since the 1970s. Some are writers and artists, others are involved in crafts, cheese-making or run small restaurants or bed and breakfasts. Others have taken up traditional forms of farming. In general, these newcomers have contributed positively to the local community, respecting its old-fashioned values, while opening it up to fresh ideas. The quality of work in the area's art and craft galleries should come as a pleasant surprise.

More and more visitors are discovering in the southwest a place where the pace of life is gentle and kind, the air clean, the scenery unspoilt and the roads relatively traffic-free. The growth in visitors has corresponded with a decline in the viability of traditional small-scale agriculture, so that many small farmers and fishermen, encouraged again by EU grants, are now diversifying into, say, bed and breakfast accommodation, farm holidays or game angling operations. The price of success is evident in July and August when the more popular towns like Schull, Kinsale and Dingle are introduced to phenomena such as traffic gridlock and shortage of parking spaces, while traffic on the Ring of Kerry and around the Lakes of Killarney proceeds nose to tail at a stately pace as cyclists, walkers and recreational vehicles all vie for space on the narrow roads. Come outside those months to appreciate the quiet charms of the mild southwest.

Having been declining steadily for more than 150 years, the rural population of Cork is now stable, while that of Kerry is actually growing. Tourism, and the jobs it produces both directly and indirectly, is partly responsible.

Fishing for a living

Historical Highlights

6000BC First traces of Stone Age man in Ireland.

2000BC First traces of Bronze Age man. The Celtic La Tène civilisation reaches Ireland.

AD1–500 Building of hill forts and ring forts.

500–800 Early Christian period; widespread monastic activity in the region.

9th century Viking invasion. Monasteries especially targeted for pillaging.

1014 Brian Boru defeats the Vikings.

1169 Norman invasion.

1537 Henry VIII orders the dissolution of the Irish monasteries.

1556 Elizabeth I of England 'plants' Munster with loyal Englishmen, including the poet Edmund Spenser and Walter Raleigh.

1580 Spanish, Italian and English supporters are defeated with Irish rebels at Dún an Óir in Dingle. Spenser is among those who massacred the defeated.

1601 Spanish and Irish forces defeated by the English at the Battle of Kinsale.

1649–52 Widespread destruction by Oliver Cromwell's army.

1689 James II lands in Kinsale with French support to reclaim his throne.

1690 William of Orange's army arrives at Kinsale following its victory at the Battle of the Boyne and attacks Charles Fort, which holds out for King James.

1796 Wolfe Tone attempts to land a French army in Bantry Bay, but is foiled by bad weather.

1798 Crushing of United Irishmen's rebellion.

1800 The Act of Union unites the British and Irish parliaments at Westminster.

1829 Daniel O'Connell's Catholic Emancipation Bill carried.

1845–50 Failure of potato crop gives rise to the Great Famine, during which 1 million die and a further 2 million emigrate.

1849 The Cove of Cork is named Queenstown in honour of the visit of Queen Victoria and Prince Albert.

1875 Parnell becomes leader of the Home Rule Movement.

1885 Home Rule is defeated in the House of Lords.

1912 The Irish National Volunteers is formed to support Home Rule.

1916 Irish rebels defeated in the Easter Rising.

1919 Guerrilla war between the IRA and the British irregulars, the Black and Tans.

1921 Britain and Ireland sign a treaty granting Dominion status to most of Ireland, with six counties of Ulster remaining part of the United Kingdom.

1922–23 Civil war between pro- and anti-partitionists. Michael Collins assassinated at Béal na Bláth, near Macroom.

1939–45 Ireland remains neutral in World War II.

1953 The last residents leave the Blasket Islands for a new life on the mainland.

1961 Television in the form of RTE1 reaches most of Cork and Kerry.

1969 'The Troubles' flare up again in Northern Ireland.

1973 Ireland joins the European Community, now European Union.

1991 Mary Robinson is elected President of Ireland.

1998–9 The historic Good Friday Agreement (1998) leads to an all-party assembly in Northern Ireland.

2002 Republic adopts the euro.

2004 President Mary MacAleese returns unopposed for a second term of office.

2005 Cork city designated European Capital of Culture.

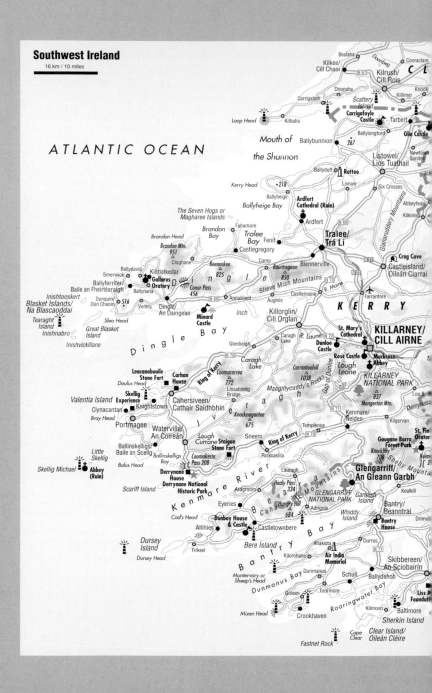

Southwest Ireland

16 km / 10 miles

ATLANTIC OCEAN

Mouth of the Shannon

Bealaha
Kilkee/ Cill Chaoi
Kilrush/ Cill Rois
Cooraclare
C L
Doonbeg
Carrigaholt
Killimer
Doonaha
Scattery Island
Carrigafoyle Castle
Knock
Kilbaha
Loop Head
Ballylongford
Tarbert
Glin Castle
Ballybunnion
267
Listowel/ Lios Tuathail
Newtown Sandes
Kerry Head
Ballyheige
Ballyduff
Rattoo
Lixnaw
Six Crosses
Kilkinlea
Ballyheige Bay
Ardfert Cathedral (Ruin)
N 69
Ardfert
Kilfenora
The Seven Hogs or Magharee Islands
Fahamore
Tralee Bay
Fenit
Tralee/ Trá Lí
Crag Cave
Brandon Head
Brandon Bay
Castlegregory
Camp
Blennerville
N 21
Castleisland/ Oileán Ciarraí
Brandon Mtn. 951
Cloghane
Beenoskee 825
Baurtregaun 850
N 23
Ballydavid
Kilmalkedar
Conor Pass 456
Slieve Mish Mountains
R. Maine
Farranfore
K E R R Y
Smerwick
Gallarus Oratory
D i n g l e
Ballynana
Camp
Aughils
Castlemaine
Ballyferriter
Baile an Fheirtéaraigh
Dunquin/ Dún Chaoin
516
Ventry
Dingle/ An Daingean
Annascaul
Inch
Killorglin/ Cill Orglan
St. Mary's Cathedral
N 72
KILLARNEY/ CILL AIRNE
Inishtooskert
Blasket Islands/ Na Blascaoddai
Slea Head
Minard Castle
Caragh Lake
Dunloe Castle
Ross Castle
Muckross Abbey
Tearaght Island
Inishnabro
Great Blasket Island
Dingle Bay
Glenbeigh
R. Laune
Lough Leane
KILLARNEY NATIONAL PARK
Inishvickillane
Caragh Lake
Carrantuohill 1038
Maegillycuddy's Reeks
Gap of Dunloe
837
Mangerton Mtn.
Loo Br
Derrynas
Leacanabuaile Stone Fort
Carhan House
Ring of Kerry
Coomacarrea 772
Kenmare/ Neiden
Kilgarvan
Doulus Head
Skellig Experience
Lissatinnig Bridge
I v e r a g h
Templenoe
St. Fin Orator
Valentia Island
Cahersiveen/ Cathair Saidhbhin
Knocknagantee 675
Gougane Barra Forest Park
Keim
Clynacantan
Knightstown
Sneem
Ring of Kerry
N 70
Knockboy 706
Sleiv Mounta
Bray Head
Portmagee
Waterville/ An Coireán
Lough Currane
Staigue Stone Fort
Parknasilla
Glengarriff/ An Gleann Garbh
Little Skellig
Ballinskelligs/ Baile an Sceilg
Ballinskelligs Bay
Coomakesta Pass 208
Lauragh
Kealkill
Skellig Michael
Abbey (Ruin)
Bolus Head
Derrynane House
Derrynane National Historic Park
Kenmare River
Healy Pass 334
GLENGARRIFF NATIONAL PARK
Garinish Island
Bantry/ Beanntrai
Scariff Island
Cod's Head
Ardgroom
Hungry Hill 684
Adrigole
Whiddy Island
Bantry House
Drimol
Eyeries
B e a r a
Dunboy House & Castle
Castletownbere
M o u n t a i n s
Durrus
N 71
Dursey Island
Allihies
Firkeel
Bere Island
Bantry Bay
Air India Memorial
Skibbereen/ An Sciobairín
Dursey Head
Muntervary or Sheep's Head
Ahakista
Kilcrohane
Dunmanus
Dunmanus Bay
Schull
Ballydehob
Liss Foundati
Goleen
Toormore
Roaringwater Bay
Kilmoon
Baltimore
Mizen Head
Crookhaven
Sherkin Island
Cape Clear
Clear Island/ Oileán Cléire
Fastnet Rock

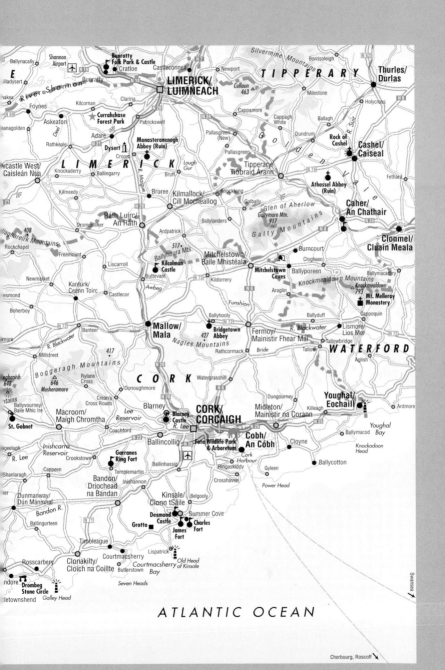

ATLANTIC OCEAN

Cork City & Environs

1. Cork Harbour East

The east side of Cork Harbour is dominated by Cobh and its cathedral. Nearby Fota Island is a sheltered environment with an arboretum and a Wildlife Park. The Queenstown Story recreates the experience of the 2.5 million people who emigrated from Cobh in the 19th and 20th centuries. The town itself, including its beautifully sited cathedral, can be explored on foot. Inland, Midleton is a market town famous for its whiskey distillery. Allow a full day. *See pullout map*

Cork Harbour

—The east side of Cork Harbour is formed by three islands, Little Island, Fota Island and Great Island, all of which are connected by causeways. Cobh is also serviced by train from Kent Station (tel: 021-450 6766 for information). If you choose to take the 25-minute train journey, you will be able to enjoy some wonderful harbour views on the way.—

Cobh is clearly signposted off the main N25 Waterford-Rosslare road, about 19km/12 miles outside Cork city. If approaching from Kinsale or West Cork, follow signs for Ringaskiddy Ferryport, turning left off the Ringaskiddy road at the sign for the Cross-River Ferry, or follow the N28 north to the tunnel.

The road from Cork brings you past the walls of the 315-hectare (780-acre) **Fota Estate**. **Fota Wildlife Park** (mid-March to October, Monday to Saturday 10am–6pm, Sunday 11am–6pm; weekends only November to mid-March, to 3pm) was created with the aim of breeding certain species that are under threat in the wild. Giraffe, zebra, ostrich, oryx and antelope roam freely in grassland, monkeys swing through trees on lake islands, while kangaroos, wal-

Fota cheetahs cuddle up

labies, lemurs and peacocks and hens have complete freedom of the park. Fota is the world's leading breeder of cheetahs, one of the few animals here that must be caged. **Fota House** (April to September daily 10am–5.30pm; October to March daily 11am–4pm) was built in the mid-18th century as a shooting lodge, and enlarged in 1820 to a symmetrical neo-classical design. Main attractions of the interior are the formal plasterwork in the reception rooms, and a tour of the kitchen and servants' quarters. There is also a tea room and craft shop. The gardens (daily 10am–5pm) include an extensive arboretum of mature trees and shrubs from China, Japan, Australia and the Himalayas, many of them rare; a fernery; an Italian rose garden; and an orangery.

Turn right out of the gates of Fota and cross Belvelly Bridge, the causeway on to Great Island. This is marked by a ruined castle, Belvelly, and just beyond it a circular Martello tower, one of many built around the coast in the early 19th century as defence against possible invasion by Napoleonic forces. About 500m (½ mile) beyond the castle **Hederman's Smoke House** offers the chance to see additive-free salmon, mussels, eel, cod and haddock being smoked over beechwood chips in the old style, and to taste and buy the excellent results.

Cobh (pronounced *Cove*) was a small fishing village, referred to as the Cove of Cork, and virtually unknown until the early 1800s. It grew in importance as a British naval base during the American Civil War, when its value as a natural deep-water harbour was first recognised.

Cobh was renamed **Queenstown** when it became the site of Queen Victoria's landing on Irish soil in 1849. It reverted to a phonetic Irish spelling of its original name after Independence in 1922.

Most of Cobh's buildings are solid and Victorian in style, dating from about 1830 to 1900. Its heyday came when its strategic position with regard to transatlantic traffic was recognised. Cobh be-

St Colman's granite cathedral behind the harbour

came the last – and first – European port of call for transatlantic shipping. Between 1848 and 1950 about 2.5 million adults and children emigrated through the port of Cobh. Their transport ranged from the notorious 'coffin ships' of the famine years – overcrowded and unseaworthy – to the relative luxury of liners belonging to the White Star and the Cunard lines. Cobh was the last port of call of the *Titanic* in 1912, and it was to here that most of the bodies recovered from the torpedoing of the *Lusitania* in 1915 were brought.

These, and other happier events in Cobh's history, are enlarged upon in **The Queenstown Story** (daily 10am–6pm). Even if you do not normally enjoy heritage centres, this one is something different. It is located in the actual railway station and customs hall that was used by the emigrants. There is a deep-water berth right alongside, which is still used by visiting cruise ships.

Cobh itself is an interesting and atmospheric town. Tourist information and art exhibitions can be found in the **Sirius Centre** next door to The Queenstown Story. This lovely waterside Palladian villa was originally the home of the Royal Cork Yacht Club, founded in 1720.

Continue walking along the seafront, then take a left, heading for the cathedral. Enjoy the ingenuity of the Victorian architecture of Cobh as you climb the steep streets lined with terraced houses built at precipitous angles. A large, Gothic-revival church, **St. Colman's Cathedral**, was built in granite between 1868 and 1915. Its spire has a carillon of 47 bells, which ring out over the harbour at 9am, noon, 4pm and 6pm daily. On the cathedral parapet, you can enjoy the view of the harbour with Haulbowline Island immediately ahead, next to the smaller Spike Island. Roches Point in the east marks Cork Harbour's entrance.

If a one-hour guided boat trip around the harbour appeals, descend again to the water's edge, and head for the quay beyond the post office. This is the embarkation point for **Marine Transport** (June to September daily at 10am, 11am, noon, 1.30pm and 2.30pm).

Telling The Queenstown Story

If you're travelling by car, head inland to the N25 for **Midleton**, a pleasant market town about 19km (12 miles) east of Cork city, with some attractive 18th-century houses and interesting artisan food shops. The Saturday morning Farmer's Market attracts visitors from miles around, and is usually enlivened by a jazz trio. Midleton is best known as the home of Jameson Irish Whiskey, and the big attraction is the **Old Midleton Distillery** (daily 10am–4.30pm last tour; November to February: daily tours at 11.30am, 2.30pm and 4pm). The tour explains the distilling process, and the massive site includes some impressive industrial architecture, notably the old waterwheel dating from 1825, and the largest pot still in the world, a massive copper dome with a capacity of 146,000 litres (32,000 gallons). But the moment most people are waiting for comes at the very end: the whiskey tasting session. There is also a restaurant, gift and craft shop.

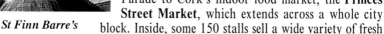

2. A Walking Tour of Cork

Cork's city centre is such a compact place that the highlights can easily be absorbed in a half-day's walk. This is necessarily highly selective. Including the university campus, and other attractions to the west of the city would extend this to a full day. *See map, page 19.*

—The starting point is the Tourist Information Office (tel: 021-425 5100) on Grand Parade, where those who wish to do a more conscientious sight seeing job can pick up a Cork City Area Guide which details further points of interest.—

Take a look across the street in front of the Tourist Information Office at a terrace of three elegant Georgian houses with slate-hung, bow-fronted windows, which recall the 18th-century prime of Cork.

In the west, across the south channel of the River Lee, you can see the spires of **St Finn Barre's Cathedral**, where the city began as a monastic school in about AD650. Both the Gothic, late-19th-century cathedral, and the bridge across the Lee are built of white limestone, a characteristic Cork building material. The grand, richly ornamented cathedral exterior, designed by William Burges in 1861, leads to a surprisingly small interior.

Leaving the river behind, walk along the Grand Parade to Cork's indoor food market, the **Princes Street Market**, which extends across a whole city

St Finn Barre's

block. Inside, some 150 stalls sell a wide variety of fresh food, ranging from traditional meat and seafood to organic vegetables and hand-made Irish cheeses. Note the stall at the door with a display of tripe (cow's intestines) and drisheen (blood sausage). This, and more tempting local specialities, can be sampled at the far end of the market in its first floor Farmgate Café, one of the city's liveliest lunch spots.

The green space in Grand Parade is **Bishop Lucey Park**, the only park in the city centre. Inside its gates is a fragment of the medieval city wall. A narrow pedestrian alley beyond it leads to the **Triskel Arts Centre**, a hub of the city's cultural life. Turn right at the west end of the alley into North Main Street, noting the restored façade of the classical **Court House**. The **Cork Vision Centre** is located in a deconsecrated Georgian church in the heart of what was once the city's medieval quarter. A 1:500 scale model of the

An afternoon in Cork

city will greatly aid your orientation. The name *Corcaigh* in Irish means 'marshy place'. The city is partly built on an island formed by two branches of the River Lee, and consequently has a confusingly large number of bridges and quays.

Retrace your steps to the Grand Parade and turn into the graceful curve of **Patrick Street**, Cork's main shopping area. The distinctive lamp standards and paving, designed by Catalan architect, Beth Galí, were installed just prior to 2005, when Cork City was designated European Capital of Culture, the smallest city ever to hold the title. Brown Thomas, halfway down the street on the right, is the most upmarket department store, and has a good range of Irish crystal, while Roches Stores, just beyond it, is the biggest store in town. At the river end of Patrick Street on Merchant's Quay there is a shopping mall with all the usual high-street stores, including Marks & Spencer.

About 20 metres along the street on the left-hand side a pedestrian alleyway next to The Body Shop leads to **Rory Gallagher Piazza**, a small pedestrianised square popular with buskers. Here an old part of Cork known as the Huguenot Quarter, named after the French Protestants who lived here in the 18th century, meets a new shopping development. This is the closest Cork gets to a 'left bank', with a cluster of antiques shops, bookstores, design-conscious home furnishing stores, fashion boutiques and trendy restaurants.

Turn right on to Paul Street for the **Crawford Municipal Gallery** (Monday to Friday 9am–5pm, Saturday 9am–1pm). If you only have time to look at one museum in the southwest, this stately Victorian edifice, which has the best public art collection outside Dublin, is the one to choose. The red-brick building incorporates the city's Custom House (1724), an octagonal turret from a later building, and a modern extension by Eric van Egeraat, added in 2001. Its collection is unusually good, featuring work by James Barry, William Orpen, Sean Keating, William Leech, Louis le Broquy, Tony O'Malley and a special display dedicated to the stained-glass artist,

Princes Street Market

Harry Clarke. It also mounts exciting contemporary exhibitions, and like all good museums, it has an excellent café.

The **Cork Opera House**, adjoining the Crawford Gallery, dates from the 1960s, but had a new façade and piazza added in 2004, where Cork's skateboarders congregate. The Opera House has events ranging from dance and drama to concerts and comedy nights. Cross the bridge in front of the Opera House, and climb the hill to the **Firkin Crane Centre**. Part of the Firkin Crane, a classical rotunda attractively built in limestone, is used for dance performances, and part of it houses the **Shandon Craft Market**. In the 18th century, when

the Firkin Crane was built, much of Cork's wealth derived from the exporting of butter. Butter was originally packed in wooden firkins, which were weighed here by crane, hence the name. Next door, the **Cork Butter Museum** (May to September Monday to Saturday 10am–5pm) explains the butter trade.

Across the road is **St Anne's Church** (May to October Monday to Saturday 9.30am–5pm; November to April Monday to Saturday 10am–3.30pm), whose steeple is known as the **Shandon**

Shandon Steeple

Steeple, and has a four-sided clock. This is a famous landmark that can be seen from most of the inner city. It is also known as the four-faced liar, as the clock often tells a different time on each side. For a small fee, you can climb the tower and attempt to ring a tune on the bells.

A further walking tour from Grand Parade heads west up Washington Street to the main campus of **University College**, Cork, known locally as UCC (daily 9am–5pm), about a ten-minute walk. The college, which has a student body of about 11,000, is part of the National University of Ireland. The main quadrangle, built in the 19th century is in the Tudor-Gothic style. On its north side several ancient stones, inscribed in the old Irish alphabet, are on display. The **Honan Collegiate Chapel**, to the east of the quadrangle, was built in 1916 in the 12th-century Hiberno-Romanesque style, and is furnished in the Celtic Revival style, with 12 stained-glass windows by Harry Clarke. Several large modern buildings have been successfully integrated into the campus, including the Boole Library, named for the college's most famous ex-alumnus, George Boole (1815–64), creator of Boolean algebra, which laid the foundations of modern computing. The **Lewis Glucksman Gallery** dates from 2004, and is an architectural gem, built on the site of a pair of tennis courts in a wooded glen beside the main gates. It has already won several presitigious awards for its architects, O'Donnell-Tuomey.

As well as displaying works from the college's collection of contemporary art, it holds interesting temporary art exhibits.

Leave the campus by the main gates and cross Western Road to reach the **Mardyke Walk**, a riverside walk famous for its cricket ground. Cricket is a minority sport in Ireland, a legacy of British occupation, played chiefly in Dublin and Cork and a few smaller towns. The walk leads to Fitzgerald Park, a pleasant riverside spot, and the location of **Cork Public Museum** (Monday to Friday 11am–5pm, Sunday 3pm–5pm). This is housed in a Georgian mansion with a modern extension, and concentrates on Cork's history and archaeology from 2000BC, with a strong emphasis on its early 20th-century Republican history.

Cross the River Lee on a pedestrian bridge known locally as the Shakey Bridge and climb up the hill, following signposts to **Cork City Gaol** (daily 9.30am–5pm, 10am–4pm November to February). This magnificent Victorian building represented 'enlightened' penal ideas when it was designed in 1824. It is peopled by waxworks, and its history is presented in a lively, accessible manner. In the same building is the **Radio Museum** (same hours), a restored Radio Studio, 6CK, the broadcast codename for Cork, dating from 1927. It was sited in a wing of the gaol because the building's location, on a ridge above the city, aided broadcasting. From here it is about ten minutes' walk to the city centre via **Sunday's Well Road**, a leafy residential area whose largely Victorian houses back on to the river, and the **North Mall**, a riverside terrace of town houses which has some of the city's most attractive domestic Georgian architecture.

3. Kinsale and District

Cork may be Ireland's second-largest city, and the capital of the county, but Kinsale, a small, historic seaport 29km (18 miles) to the south of the city, is the big attraction for most visitors. Allow a full day. *See map, page 26*

–From the airport, turn right for Kinsale at the exit instead of turning left for Cork. Kinsale is 20 minutes' drive from the airport, and about half an hour from the city centre on the R600.–

Up until the late 1970s, Kinsale was a small, run-down fishing port that had never recovered economically from the sudden departure of the British Army after the War of Independence in 1922. In spite of its sheltered location on the estuary of the Bandon River, with a large fjord-like harbour running southwest to the open sea, Kinsale remained resolutely

On the bright side, Kinsale

Kinsale harbour

run-down. Its tall, elegant Georgian houses were in a state of dilapidation, the streets were potholed and there was not a single restaurant in town.

Nowadays, you can choose from over a dozen ambitious and innovative restaurants. The houses are carefully maintained and brightly painted, many of them enhanced by floral displays and window boxes. Yachting and deep-sea angling have become popular seasonal activities, operating from two marinas. Property values are among the highest in the country. While most west Cork towns are twinned with their Brittany equivalent, Kinsale is twinned with sunny Antibes–Juan les Pins.

Wander around and sample the atmosphere. Interesting craft shops, art galleries, food shops and antiques emporia well outnumber tatty souvenir vendors. Kinsale may be more expensive than the rest of the southwest, but it certainly has style. There is an easy-going, cosmopolitan atmosphere that is generally absent from the typical Irish small town.

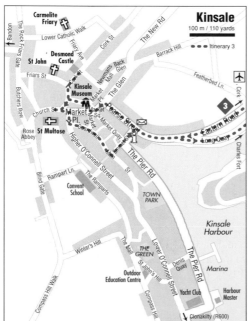

The Battle of Kinsale in 1601 is often referred to as a turning point in Irish history. The Irish, and the Spanish, who had come to the aid of their Catholic allies, were resoundingly defeated by the forces of Queen Elizabeth I of England. It was the last great stand of Gaelic and Catholic Ireland; the Earls left for France and Spain soon afterwards, and were replaced by noblemen loyal to the English crown and religion.

The **Old Courthouse** in Market Square dates from 1600. In 1706, a Dutch-style gabled frontage and octagonal clock tower were added. The walls are faced with slates, an architectural feature called weather-slating which is characteristic of 18th-century houses in County Cork. The slating was used as much for decoration as for weather-proofing.

The Courthouse now contains the **Kinsale Regional Museum** (Easter–October daily 10.30am–4pm, November–Easter Wednesday to Sunday only), whose exhibits include mementos of the wreck of the ill-fated transatlantic passenger liner, the *Lusitania*. A German submarine sunk this ship 23km (14 miles) off the coast of the Old Head of Kinsale in 1916. This action, in which 1,198 passengers and crew were killed, caused such outrage that it brought the United States into the Great War.

Two minutes' walk from the museum is **Desmond Castle** (mid-June–mid-October daily 10am–6pm, mid-April–mid-June Tuesday to Sunday only), a 16th-century tower house which has recently been restored. It was used as a prison during the 18th century, and is still known locally as 'the French Prison'. It currently houses an exhibit celebrating wine-producing families of Irish origin.

The building behind the walls at the bottom of the hill is **St Multose Church**, which is the parish church of the Church of Ireland, parts of which date from the 13th century. Note the massive stone-built West Tower.

It takes about 45 minutes to walk out of town to Charles Fort, following signs for the **Scilly Walk**. Part of the way is a wooded, waterside footpath with excellent views across the harbour.

Charles Fort (mid-March to October

Charles Fort

daily 10am–6pm; November to mid-March: Saturday and Sunday 10am–5pm) is a star-shaped structure enclosing 3.6 hectares (9 acres) of ground, and was built in 1677. Because it is overlooked by high ground on the landward side, and is therefore vulnerable to attack from the land, it was not a great success militarily. For most of its working life, which ended when the IRA burnt it down in 1921, it was used as a recruit training centre. There is good cut-stone work on many of the buildings, and wonderful sea views from its bastions.

If you walked out to the fort, you can break your return journey at the inexpensive Bulman Bar in Summer Cove which serves bar food, or wait until you reach the town centre and try the delicious local seafood in Fishy Fishy, one of ireland's leading seafood restaurants.

Ballinspittle madonna

Leave town by crossing the River Bandon. Follow the scenic route signposted **Old Head of Kinsale**. The land at the extremity of the Old Head has been a private golf club since 1997, so unfortunately there is no longer any access for walkers.

Turn left when leaving the Old Head, and drive past two sandy beaches at **Garretstown**. Turn right at the end of the second beach to the village of **Ballinspittle**, a small agricultural hamlet, chiefly remarkable for its **Grotto**. Like many other shrines to Our Lady in the country, this was built in the Marian year (a year of special devotion to the Virgin Mary), 1954. In the summer of 1985, it achieved worldwide fame when thousands of people claimed they saw the statue move, and pilgrims flocked to Ballinspittle. A religious fundamentalist smashed the statue at the end of the summer, and the replacement is apparently static, although the people of the village still live in hope.

4. Blarney Castle

A visit to Blarney Castle makes a pleasant half-day outing. Do not be put off by Blarney's reputation as a tourist trap. The crowds are easily absorbed by the spacious gardens that surround the castle, as well as by the numerous sweater and craft shops around the village. *See map, pages 16–17*

–The main reason for visiting Blarney is to see a splendid example of an Irish castle – in fact, a castle keep or tower house.–

Blarney Castle (October to April Monday to Saturday 9am–sundown; May to September 9.30am–6.30pm) is not actually furnished, but neither, like many castles of its age, is it a ruin. All the rooms that make up a fortified 16th-century home are intact, and can be visited. In addition, there are some 160 hectares (400 acres) of gardens, intersected by two rivers, surrounding the castle.

Blarney Castle was built by Dermot Macarthy, a local clan chieftain in the mid-15th century. It is 26m (85ft) tall, with walls that are in places 6m (18ft) thick, and is one of the largest castles in the country.

Kissing the Blarney Stone

Like most castles of this era, it was built on high ground in a strategically important position near a source of fresh water. It was basically a fortified home. Above the narrow entrance lobby is a removable stone, known as a murder hole, which enabled those holding the castle to pour boiling oil, or to aim musket fire, on to intruders. The staircase is narrow so that it can be defended by one man holding a sword. While there is only one slit window at ground level, the windows get larger as you climb higher, and they become much less vulnerable to attack.

Central to a visit to Blarney Castle lies the ritual of kissing the **Blarney Stone**, which is supposed to bestow the gift of eloquence. The word 'blarney' has entered the English language to mean smoothly flattering or cajoling talk. It is believed to have originated as a description of the excuses made to England's Queen Elizabeth I by the then Lord Blarney, who was reluctant to hand his castle over to the Crown.

To reach the stone first you must climb 120 steep stone steps through the five storeys of the castle. The stone is located right at the top, on a parapet which is open to the sky, and was originally used as a look-out. A great view of the wooded Lee Valley rewards your climb.

To kiss the stone you must lie on your back while an attendant holds on to you, and drop your head backwards and downwards. There is no charge, but most people give the attendant a euro coin. The castle authorities assure visitors that the stone is disinfected at regular intervals, and there is no danger of infection.

Wander through the gardens afterwards, and explore the strangely shaped limestone rocks, and a grove of ancient yew trees which are said to have Druidic connections.

The other thing to do at Blarney is shop for local crafts. Blarney Woollen Mills claims to be the biggest sweater shop in the country, and has some attractive bargains in among the kitsch. If you want to compare prices, there are other craft shops within a short walk.

If you like industrial architecture, you can return to Cork via Ballincollig on the main Cork-Killarney road (N22), and take a look at the recently restored **Royal Gunpowder Mills** (April to September daily except Saturday 10am–5pm). In the 19th century, gunpowder for the armies of the British Empire was manufactured here, and the workers lived in constant fear of an explosion. The River Lee was diverted into a canal system and there is a working 'Incorporating Mill' which is powered by a water wheel.

The N22 will take you right into Cork city.

Blarney Castle

5. Gateway to the Southwest

This full-day excursion consists of a leisurely drive from the airport to Skibbereen, the heart of scenic west Cork. The R600 follows the edge of Courtmacsherry Bay. Clonakilty has many features typical of west Cork's towns and villages, including brightly painted shop fronts with wooden windows. This contrasts with the unspoilt wilderness of the long sandy beaches nearby at Inchydoney, while Glandore's deep-water harbour attracts yachts from near and far. *See pullout map*

Franciscan Friary

—Whether you are starting from the airport or from Kinsale, the journey begins by crossing the Bandon River west of Kinsale. Follow signs for the R600.—

The road runs inland for a couple of miles, emerging at the sea again at a wide sandy beach known as **Kilbrittain Strand**. The pretty, multi-coloured buildings visible across the estuary are **Courtmacsherry**, once a fishing village, now a holiday resort. The road runs along the edge of the Courtmacsherry estuary which in winter months is home to great flocks of plover, oystercatchers and curlew. In the summer, cormorants, egrets and herons should be easy to spot.

The distant view of Timoleague, a small village at the top of the estuary, is dominated by the grey stone ruins of a waterside 12th-century **Franciscan Friary**. Until the 16th century, before the estuary silted up, the monks were known as wine importers. The ruins are freely accessible through a gate on the landward side. Until quite recently, sites like these were considered prestigious places to be buried, and the atmosphere of the interior is marred by the presence of various modern graves.

The floor plan of the old abbey is clearly marked by identifying plaques. Most visitors find the tall Gothic windows framing sweeping views of the estuary and its wooded green slopes offer an irresistible photo-opportunity.

If churches interest you, check out the interior of Timoleague's tiny **Church of Ireland**, on the right where the R600 enters the village. A mosaic mural in the decorative style favoured by the Oxford Movement covers the interior walls of the church. To appreciate the gold leaf you must find someone to put on the lights; their address is usually taped inside the church door. The replica Hiberno-Romanesque-style **Church of Our Lady's Nativity** on the hill behind contains some fine stained-glass windows by the acclaimed Dublin artist Harry Clarke (1889–1931).

Continue on the R600 to **Clonakilty**. Emmet Square has some good Georgian houses. The **General Post Office** is in a small 19th-century church on the south side of the square. Beside it is **Spiller's Lane**, an attractive arcade with antiques and craft shops. As you walk around the town, note the attractive hand-painted shop signs above wooden shop fronts which have been revived in recent years.

Signposted off the town by-pass on the road to the **Model Village** (of interest chiefly to railway buffs and children – Febraury to October daily 11am–5pm) is **Inchydoney Strand**. Inchydoney was, until the mid-19th century, an island. The causeway that now links it to the mainland was one of many projects undertaken in the 1840s to provide work for those whose potato crop had failed during the Great Famine.

The large new hotel (The Lodge and Spa at Ichydoney Island) features a seawater spa; treatments can be booked by non-residents *(see page 87)*. On either side, long, sandy beaches are pounded by Atlantic rollers. If it's good walking weather, the best dunes are

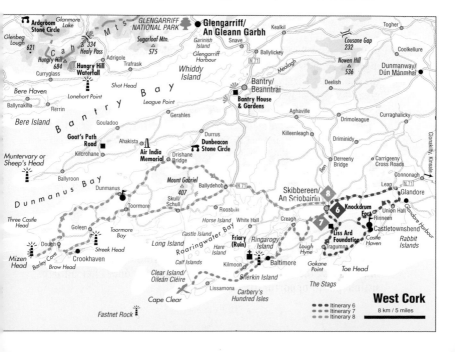

West Cork

8 km / 5 miles

Drombeg Stone Circle

situated on the left as you face the sea. Allow about 40 minutes to explore them.

Return to Clonakilty, and take the town-centre road to sample the home-made food at An Súgán (inexpensive), a rustic-style pub named after the straw-seated traditional chairs.

History enthusiasts will enjoy the quaintly old-fashioned **West Cork Regional Museum** (Monday to Saturday 10am–6pm, Sunday 3pm–6pm) which features Michael Collins memorabilia among its endearingly eclectic collection. It is on the town's main street, to the west of the impressively large Catholic church.

Continue west on the N71. A signpost on the right about 200m/yds beyond **Pike Cross**, 6km (4 miles) west of Clonakilty, leads to the **Collins Homestead** (freely accessible), the birthplace of Michael Collins. The ground plan of the farmhouse and smallholding is indicated, and there is a dignified bronze head of the controversial patriot. A further 5km (3 miles) on is **Sam's Cross**, where Collins had his last drink, and a large memorial bronze. The Four Alls, a pretty country pub, will be familiar to those who saw Neil Jordan's 1996 film, *Michael Collins*. The better-known but less attractive memorial, **Béal na Bláth**, where Collins was assassinated, is best approached from Macroom.

Return to the main road. After running through a cutting of exposed slate, the same material you see on most traditional roofs in the southwest, the N71 crosses the estuary at **Rosscarbery**. The village is on a hill up to your right. Rosscarbery was an important monastic centre from the 6th to the 12th century. The small Protestant Cathedral is no bigger than most churches. It dates from 1612, although it has been extensively and rather attractively renovated.

Turn left just outside Rosscarbery on to the R597 Glandore road. From June to September this little road, and many others like it around west Cork, are lined by tall hedges of fuchsia magellanica, a shrub with bright red, bell-shaped flowers imported from Chile in the 19th century which has adapted so well to the climate that it grows wild in

Bust of Michael Collins

profusion. In August, it is joined by bright purple heather under-growth, to create a clashing, but attractive, colourscape.

About 3km (2 miles) along is the road to the **Drombeg Stone Circle**, one of the most complete and most impressively situated of the region's early Iron Age remains. The circle is oriented to the win-ter solstice. In the rare event of a cloudless afternoon on 21 December, the last rays of the sun travel through a cut in the distant moun-tains and land on the flat stone at the far side of the circle. Beside it is a cooking pit.

For many people, including the businessman and philanthropist Tony O'Reilly who has a home here, **Glandore**, a tiny village built on the south-facing slope of a protected harbour inlet, is one of the most beautiful places in the world. Its local nickname is Mil-lionaire's Row. In winter, it is virtually empty, with a year-round population well below the 100 mark, while in summer it is teem-ing with visitors.

Stop at the top of the village and admire its wide deep-water har-bour and the lovely wooded hills that surround it. The two biggest islands in the harbour are known as Adam and Eve. The old sailing instructions for entering Glandore warn mariners to 'avoid Adam and hug Eve'. Stop for a drink in the open air at the Glandore Inn.

Rejoin the main road at **Leap**, which continues into **Skibbereen**.

6. Irish R.M. Country

This half-day tour around the coast to the southeast of Skib-bereen visits the countryside featured in the Irish R.M. stories of Somerville and Ross. It also looks at an ambitious new land-scape development, the Liss Ard Foundation. *See map, page 31*

—Take the N71 to Leap and turn off at the signpost for Union Hall, which is not a hall but a small fishing village. Note the brightly painted, multi-coloured houses which are such a feature of the area. It is said that this tradition originated because fishermen used whatever was left over from the an-nual painting of their boats to brighten up their houses.—

Castletownshend is signposted from Union Hall on an attractive back road which passes through **Rineen**, a village so small that it is barely a place at all, but most beautifully located beside a pine-clad inlet. **Ceim Hill Museum** (Monday to Sat-

At Ceim Hill Museum

urday 10am–6.30pm, Sunday 2pm–6.30pm, but telephone in advance off season, tel: 028-36280) is signposted 3km (2 miles) off this road. Owner-curator and herbalist Teresa O'Mahony will show you her col-lection of artefacts. To the untutored eye it may look like a heap

of stones, but Teresa's project has the approval of several learned professors. From her garden there is an excellent aerial view of Castlehaven, the harbour of Castletownshend.

There is only one road into **Castletownshend**. Drive down the hill and head for Mary Ann's (028-36146), one of the oldest pubs in the country. Phone ahead during off-season to confirm bar food availability; the seafood is renowned. Its low-beamed interior and paved beer garden are worth a visit at any time of day.

Castletownshend may be the prettiest village in west Cork, but it is also the least typical. Wander along its two streets, noting its large, well designed three- and four-storey houses, often stone-built and neoclassical in style. These belonged to members of a group of intermarried 'planter' families – Protestant settlers, often former English soldiers – who were awarded lands in the area in the late 17th century. The intention was to 'plant' this remote area with people who would be loyal to the Crown in the event of an uprising. The families prospered as merchants, and in many cases their descendants still live here.

A wall plaque in **St Barrahane's Church**, which is reached by climbing 52 stone steps, enlarges on the history of the planter families. There are also three interesting stained-glass windows by the Dublin artist Harry Clarke.

Behind this church, which dates from 1826, are the graves of Edith Somerville (1858–1949) and her writing partner, Violet Martin (1862–1915). As **Somerville and Ross**, they are best known for a series of comic sketches of Irish country life, *Some Experiences of an Irish R.M.* (the initials stand for Resident Magistrate), in which clever but devious locals consistently get the better of a good-natured Englishman. They also wrote travel sketches and a well-regarded novel, *The Real Charlotte*. Edith served as the organist at St Barrahane's for 70 years. Her gravestone is an uncut hunk of local slate. There is a wonderful view of the sheltered anchorage from the grave.

Liss Ard Foundation

Return to the top of the village and turn left. This road meanders along the coast past a small promontory, Toe Head. The road around Toe Head itself is best explored on foot as there are good views in all directions. There are small rocky coves with safe bathing hidden in the cliffs. The only place with any facilities (toilets, pub) is **Tragumna**, a safe sandy beach facing a small island.

The road back to Skibbereen (R596) brings you to the gates of the **Liss Ard Foundation** (Monday to Friday 10am–4pm, except public holidays) about a mile outside the town. If you have an hour or two to spare this unusual garden is well worth visiting. Some 80 hectares (200 acres) of woodlands, meadows, lakes and waterfalls are being developed to display Irish nature at its best. The garden is designed to encourage quiet contemplation. The paths lead to naturally framed prospects, and encourage Zen-like contemplation of these vistas from strategically placed benches. The most exciting bit is the Sky Garden, designed by the American artist James Turrell, where you lie on your back on a stone plinth in a crater watching clouds race across the sky. It's a strange, disorienting experience which people either love or hate. Continue on the R596 to Skibbereen.

7. West of Skibbereen

The Skibbereen Heritage Centre, Lough Ine, the coastal village of Baltimore and the nearby Sherkin Island can be visited in a half day. However, if you intend going to Cape Clear Island, an Irish-speaking bird-watcher's paradise, allow a whole day. *See map, page 31*

–Skibbereen is a traffic-choked market town built in a bourgeois style in the 19th and early 20th centuries. It has an excellent supermarket, Fields Super Valu, the place to fill up a picnic basket.–

The Heritage Centre, on Upper Bridge Street (mid-May to mid-September daily 10am–6pm; mid-March to mid-May and mid-September to November Tuesday to Saturday 10am–6pm) commemorates the Great Famine of 1845–47 which took the lives of over 10,000 people in Skibbereen. The centre also introduces the marine life of nearby Lough Ine.

Lough Ine (also spelt Hyne) is signposted to the left about 5km (3 miles) down the Baltimore road (R595). The landlocked salt water lake is a marine reserve with many unusual species. Its high wooded shores and sheltered location give it a very special atmosphere. To my mind, Lough Ine is the most peaceful place on this coast, close to heaven if you have it to yourself on a sunny day. There is good deep-water swimming off the pier, and the water is usually a few degrees warmer than the open sea.

Lough Ine

35

Avoid touching the bottom of the lake, though, as it damages rare forms of life and, more pragmatically, some of the sea urchins have poisonous spines. Walk around the path on the west side of the lake to discover the narrow passage where sea rushes in at high tide.

Baltimore, 19km (12 miles) south of Skibbereen, is another end-of-the-line village, with one road in and one road out. It can be hectic in July and August. The ruined castle overlooking the harbour was an O'Driscoll stronghold before English domination.

In 1631, Baltimore was raided by pirates from Algeria, who carried off 200 of its inhabitants. Those who were left moved inland to found Skibbereen. Hence the name of the bar opposite the castle – the Algiers Inn. They have a very odd sense of humour in west Cork. Perhaps it has something to do with the long winters.

Ballydehob mermaid

Baltimore is the most accessible port of call on **Roaring Water Bay**, and is popular with boating enthusiasts. In good visibility, the **Fastnet Rock Lighthouse** can be seen on the horizon some 23km (14 miles) to the south. This tiny hamlet is also the base for the mail boats and ferries servicing Roaring Water Bay's two largest inhabited Islands, Cape Clear and Sherkin.

Sherkin Island is a quick hop from Baltimore (tel: 028-20187 for ferry details. Services run half-hourly in summer). The main activities on offer are walking, swimming or picnicking among its cliffs, strands and rocky bays. There is one pub, the Jolly Roger, and a small hotel, both serving food, and the ruins of a 15th-century Franciscan Friary.

Cape Clear is reached by a thrilling 45-minute boat ride through the rocks and shoals of Roaring Water Bay (tel: 028-28138 for ferry details. There is usually a boat out at 11am, returning at 5.30pm, weather permitting). Cape Clear is an Irish-speaking island about 5km (3 miles) long by 2km (1 mile) across, with a population of about 170. There are three pubs, a youth hostel, a bird observatory, a small heritage centre and various B&Bs. The ferry lands in the **North Harbour**. A walk to the **South Harbour** (follow signposts for the Youth Hostel) will take you to a sheltered bay. Because of its southerly position, Cape Clear's Bird Observatory often reports landings of rare migratory birds, and the appearance of large flocks. On 22 October 1990, for example, 3,500 skylarks were spotted on one day.

The other road leads to higher ground, and a freshwater lake, **Lough Errol**. Cape Clear is one of the few locations left in the country where you are likely to hear the corncrake calling. Whales and dolphins can sometimes be spotted offshore. Closer by, keep an eye out for wild goats, who might want to share your picnic.

Pause for refreshment at Bunratty Inn

8. The Mizen Peninsula

This day-long drive (105km/65 miles) takes you through the heart of scenic west Cork, and around the Mizen peninsula, providing dramatic coastal scenery to rival anything found on the entire coast of Ireland. *See map, page 31*

–The N71 west leaves Skibbereen beside the banks of the River Ilen.–

About 8km (6 miles) out of Skibbereen keep an eye out to the left for your first view of Roaring Water Bay and its numerous islands. The road turns inland again, and you leave the N71 for the R592 by keeping straight on at the entrance to **Ballydehob**. This lively, brightly painted village, apparently situated in the middle of nowhere, comes as something of a surprise. Once the marketing centre for the islanders of Roaring Water Bay, Ballydehob is nowadays a popular retreat for urban dwellers – English, Dutch, German and even Irish – seeking a better quality of life. Some have holiday homes in the area, while others have made the big leap and live here all year round.

Continue on the R592. In good weather you will be able to see **Mount Gabriel** (407m/1,335ft) on your right. The two white balls on its summit guide transatlantic air traffic. If you wake early in west Cork, you can often hear a stream of jumbo jets high above, heading for the airports of Europe.

While Ballydehob has a reputation for being arty, **Schull**, 5km (3 miles) down the R592, is the heart of fashionable west Cork. Walk down to the pier for another look at Roaring Water Bay, then explore its one main street, checking out its choice of restaurants, bookshops and craft boutiques. If you fancy a picnic, the Courtyard Delicatessen sells food, while the

Altar Rock near Schull

Mizen Head

best bar meals can be had at Bunratty Inn.

There is always a sense of leaving civilisation behind as you drive away from the fleshpots of Schull on the R592 for Goleen. The road passes rocky, rugged bits of low-lying coast. About 7km (4 miles) west at **Altar**, look out for a megalithic tomb on the left of the road, known locally as the Altar Rock *(see picture on page 37)*.

The quiet village of **Goleen** consists mainly of pubs. Take the R591 to **Crookhaven**. This tiny village is indeed a haven tucked into a crook of land. Its most famous resident was the Italian physicist Guglielmo Marconi, who set up a telegraph station here in 1902. The ruins of the telegraph station, and the open sea, can be seen by walking up the road marked 'cul de sac' for about a mile to **Brow Head**. Afterwards drop into O'Sullivan's Bar on the quay. It's patronised by lobster fishermen, and the walls are covered with portraits of local characters.

Back on the mainland, turn left instead of right and climb up a steep hill past **Barley Cove**. This is the best sandy beach in the area, backed by dunes and with a hotel complete with a pitch-and-putt golf course.

At the T-junction, turn left for **Mizen Head**. This is a dramatic spot, with wild Atlantic waves pounding the rocks even in the calmest weather. The lighthouse signal has been automatic, and the station unattended, since 1993. The **Mizen Vision** (June to September daily 10.30am–5.30pm; October to May 11am–5pm; November to March weekends noon–4pm) is located in the lighthouse keeper's house on an island at the tip of the peninsula. To reach it you must cross a concrete suspension bridge while the waves swirl around 50 metres/yds below. Don't forget your camera.

Characterful O'Sullivan's Bar

Afterwards return to Barley Cove and turn left beyond the hotel. As the road slopes towards sea level you will see the square shell of **Dunmanus Castle** ahead, a three-storey structure piled up on a rocky outcrop. The castle was built by the O'Mahonys in the 15th century.

Now continue your journey along the R591, noting how the vegetation becomes more lush as the shore of **Dunmanus Bay** becomes more sheltered. A right turn at Drishane Bridge will take you around the back of Mount Gabriel to Ballydehob and the N71 running back to Skibbereen.

Bantry Bay & the Beara

9. The Essential Bantry Bay

This full-day drive covers the shore of Bantry Bay, starting with a cliff-top journey to Glengarriff, where there is the option of a boat trip to the gardens of Ilnacullin. After a look at Glengarriff National Park, we return to the east side of the bay for a circular drive around Sheep's Head, Cork's smallest and most undeveloped peninsula, returning to Bantry on Goat's Path. See map, page 40

–The N71 passes by the waters of Bantry Bay before reaching the town. The bay is approximately 34km (21 miles) long and 6km (4 miles) wide.–

Bantry House (March to October: daily 10am–6pm) is this side of the town. The large, mid-18th-century mansion has a magnificent setting overlooking Bantry Bay, its islands and the mountains on the opposite shore. Walk to the top of the steps in the Italian garden behind the house for the best views. The interior will please those who complain that English stately homes have been over-restored. Bantry House, which is still privately owned, is either

Bantry House

Bantry House interior

under-restored, verging on the shabby, or full of atmosphere depending on taste.

There is a fine collection of treasures, mostly collected by the second Earl of Bantry on his European Grand Tour, including Aubusson carpets, Gobelin tapestries, Russian icons, Chinese lacquer and a mixture of French and Irish 18th-century furniture. But Bantry House isn't just a museum: for 10 days in late June it is the venue for an internationally acclaimed chamber-music festival, and one wing has been converted for B&B accommodation.

In the yard of the house is the **Bantry 1796 French Armada Exhibition Centre** (same hours, separate entrance charge), a small museum commemorating the failed attempt by Wolfe Tone and his French ally, General Hoche, to land 14,000 troops in Bantry Bay over 200 years ago. The landing was impeded by bad weather.

The N71 takes you through Bantry, a market town of about 3,000 inhabitants whose chief industry is the production of mussels. These can be sampled at O'Connor's Seafood Bar (inexpensive) in the main square. The square, which was recently renovated in an incongruous yellow brick, has a Friday morning country market which attracts not only farmers, but is also a meeting point for the alternative life-stylers, mainly English and Welsh, who have settled in the area.

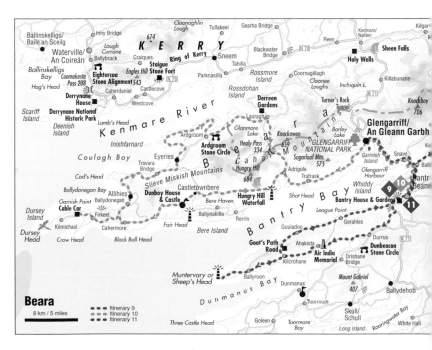

Beyond Bantry the road becomes more wooded, with intermittent views of the bay. As you drive through **Ballylickey**, a kind of leafy, waterside suburb of Bantry, look out for Manning's Emporium. The owner, Val Manning, has done an enormous amount to promote and support small local food producers in the area whose locations are shown on a mural-map. The Emporium has an excellent selection of locally made and imported cheeses, charcuterie, organic vegetables, freshly baked bread and some interesting wines on sale. Stock up now, as such things are not easy to find when you go further west.

The N71 climbs above Bantry Bay into open, more rugged country, offering ever-changing views across the bay. Pull in at one of the lay-bys to enjoy the panorama of sea, sky and mountain. The largest island in Bantry Bay is **Whiddy Island**, which is still inhabited, but is only now recovering from the *Betelgeuse* disaster in 1979 in which 50 people died when an oil tanker caught fire at the island's jetty.

Glengarriff, a wooded glen with a sheltered harbour warmed by the Gulf Stream, has an especially mild climate, with an average annual temperature of about 11°C (52°F). Azaleas, rhododendrons, magnolia, camellias, arbutus and fuchsia all grow in abundance here.

Mussel fisherman

Ilnacullin (March and October Monday to Saturday 10am–4.30pm, Sunday 1–5pm; April, May, June and September Monday to Saturday 10am–6.30pm; Sunday 1–7pm; July and August Monday to Saturday 9.30am–6.30pm, Sunday 11am–7pm), also known as Garinish Island, is worth a visit. Touts will approach your car offering boat rides. There's no need to bargain; the boats are licensed and the price for the five-minute trip is fixed (€8 return at time of writing). Wait for the second wave of touts whose boats sail from the Blue Lagoon which is the prettiest embarkation point. An added bonus in sunny weather is the sight of basking seals on the rocks between the mainland and the island.

This island of 15 hectares (37 acres) was landscaped in the early 20th century by Annan Bryce, and bequeathed to the Irish nation in 1953. Allow at least an hour and a half to walk the various paths. Perhaps the best feature of Ilnacullin is the Italian Garden, a formal creation complete with colonnades and a terrace from which the contrast between the classical man-made beauty of the garden and the wild mountain scenery that surrounds it is at its most intense.

Glengarriff village is teeming with the usual craft shops and coach parks. To picnic in more peaceful surroundings drive through the village and about 1km (½ mile) up the Kenmare road (N71) to **Glengarriff National Park**. A river and several streams run through the wooded park which, although it has picnic tables and gravel paths, is pleasantly unspoilt, and feels much more remote than it

Cottage industry

actually is. Serious walkers can pick up a leaflet in Glengarriff showing walking routes to **Barley Lake** (about 16km/10 miles round trip) and the **Sugarloaf Mountain** (575m/1,887ft).

Head back along the N71 to Bantry, enjoying views of the bay from a different angle. We suggest prolonging your tour in fine weather by driving through Bantry and back east along the N71 to the second signpost, which is labelled Sheep's Head Peninsula (ignore the first one labelled Goat's Path).

The circuit of the **Muntervary** or **Sheep's Head Peninsula** will add 68km (42 miles) and approximately two hours to the length of your day, but is worth taking for the quiet, unspoilt coastal scenery.

Beyond **Durrus**, a cheerful little village at the top of **Dunmanus Bay**, which divides the Mizen peninsula from the Sheep's Head peninsula, the road hugs the water's edge, passing through the tiny village of Ahakista, known for its minuscule, old-fashioned bar with a 'tin' (corrugated-iron) roof. If you're lucky, you might find traditional musicians having a 'session'.

The road ends 8km (5 miles) beyond **Kilcrohane**. It is worth going on and following the footpath to the lighthouse from where you can see **Bere Island** to the north, and **Mizen Head** in the south. On the return journey, you will have a good view of the snug, white-washed farmhouses that dot the countryside. Previously the homes of sheep farmers and fishermen, many are now occupied by incomers.

In Kilcrohane follow the sign for **Goat's Path**, which rises gently and then suddenly drops down to the north of the peninsula, giving a view of Bantry Bay and the Caha Mountains. If you are lucky, a setting sun will be casting a red glow over the scene. To return to Bantry you should turn left on reaching the N71.

The Allihies road

10. Ring of Beara

The Ring of Beara is less well known than the Ring of Kerry on the Iveragh Peninsula, yet it offers equally impressive scenery. The peninsula is supplied with restaurants and accommodation, but the only town of significance is Castletownbere, and the best activities are outdoor ones. It is a favourite haunt of walkers, cyclists, birdwatchers and people who enjoy uncommercialised, natural beauty. Although the drive is only about **110km (68 miles)**, much of it is on narrow, winding roads, so allow a full day. *See map, page 40*

—The Beara Peninsula stretches for about 48km (30 miles) southwest from Kenmare and Glengarriff, forming the north side of Bantry Bay. The Caha and Slieve Miskish mountains run down the centre of the peninsula, and the road around it is on a narrow coastal plain.—

The gateway to the Beara is Glengarriff. There is a great sense of relief at turning one's back on the busy tourist village and heading down the R572 to a quieter, less self-consciously beautiful place. Almost at once bungalows and B&B signs disappear to be replaced by heathland and sheep.

Adrigole offers access to the Healy Pass, a simple but impressive feat of engineering which cuts across the peninsula connecting Adrigole in County Cork with the village of Lauragh in County Kerry. It is generally accepted that the views from the Healy Pass are better travelling from north to south, and so we will save that route for the end of the day.

Hungry Hill, a conical mountain which at 684m (2,244 ft) is the highest of the Caha mountains, is signposted just beyond Adrigole, and has a 60-m (200-ft) high waterfall running down the seaward side. On my last visit, the road ended at an abandoned car on which are painted the words 'Park Here'. The waterfall is about 20 minutes' boggy walking across a beautiful empty valley.

Return to the main road, and keep an eye out to the left for Bere Island, the largest island in Bantry Bay,

Ferry ahead

View at Dzogchen Beara Retreat

which forms the sheltered harbour of Berehaven. This magnificent deep-water harbour is chiefly used by Russian factory ships which moor here and buy from local trawlers. It is not unusual to find 60 or more of them anchored here in the spring.

This also explains why there are sometimes notices in Cyrillic script pinned up in Castletownbere's supermarket. Many would consider the town, with a population of 850, little more than a village. It has an exceptionally attractive location, nestling underneath the Slieve Miskish mountains, facing the blue waters of Bantry Bay, but nobody could claim the town is a thing of beauty.

It is a busy working port, home to Ireland's largest white-fish trawling fleet. Get a feel for the place by walking along the quays and admiring its brightly coloured fleet. The quays lead to the main square and the town's one street. Most of the buildings are in a heavy Victorian style and date from the late 19th century, when Castletownbere was an important base for the British Navy, as well as a fishing port. In the square, look out for the hostelry with the words *Bar del Marinero* painted above it, a reminder that many of the boats using this port are Spanish and also French.

Leave town on the R575, turning left after about 5km (3 miles) at **Dunboy**. There are some short but very attractive walks along the shoreline and around the grounds of Dunboy, which is a small, wooded peninsula. There are two 'castles' here. The first, more picturesque ruin, is the remains of **Dunboy House**, a grandiose stone mansion built in the 19th century in the Scottish baronial style by a local mining tycoon, and burnt out in 1921. This magnificent ruin was recently sold to developers, and may soon be reincarnated as a luxury hotel. At the end of the little peninsula are the badly ruined but clearly excavated remains of the original **Dunboy Castle**. This was built in the 16th century or possibly earlier by the O'Sullivan clan. They retreated here after the defeat at the Battle of Kinsale in 1601, and blew it up rather than surrender to the English forces who were besieging it.

Continue west on the R572. The sky, sea and mountain scenery starts to get really spectacular. For a closer look at the coast,

Rainbow in Eyeries

follow signs for Garranes Hostel and the **Dzogchen Beara Retreat Centre**. Without disturbing the peace of the Buddhist monks who run the centre, have a look at their view of **Black Ball Head**, and if possible spend a few minutes in their breathtaking cliff-top meditation centre. You may well find yourself resolving to come back.

There are two routes to Allihies, as the next signpost will make clear. To visit **Dursey Head** at the end of the peninsula involves an extra 16km (10 miles), and is well worth it. The road ends at the cable car which connects Dursey Island, which forms the very tip of the peninsula, to the mainland. The cable car is licensed to carry three passengers or one cow. The island is still inhabited by half a dozen families, but has no pub and no shop.

Backtrack to the signpost for Allihies, and brace yourself for one of the most beautiful, if small-scale, stretches of road you will ever travel. **Allihies**, a straggle of brightly coloured cottages set between sea and hills, was originally built for the copper miners working in the hills behind it. The sandy beach at **Ballydonegan** just below the village was formed of spoil from the mines. Walk up behind the village to the mines (marked by tall brick chimneys) and enjoy the views of sea and wild hillside. You can walk from here to the next

village, Eyeries (11km/7 miles), on a 'green road' or footpath that forms part of the Beara Way. Even if you can only manage to travel a few miles of it, the peace and isolation will be unforgettable.

The road between Allihies and **Eyeries**, another village of small, brightly coloured houses, is one of the highlights of the Ring of Beara. In good weather the **Iveragh Peninsula** is clearly visible to the north, across the **Kenmare River**, as are the conical-shaped **Skellig Rocks** off its tip. Many of the small coastal

Healy Pass

settlements, where a living was made from fishing for cod, disappeared in the mid-20th century when the American market for salt cod petered out at the end of the Depression. Nowadays, long rafts can be seen in the waters of the Kenmare River on which mussels and oysters are farmed. They provide much-needed jobs.

Just beyond Ardgroom village, the **Ardgroom Stone Circle** is signposted. This is about two fields in from the road, and the walking is fairly rough. It is one of the most complete of the Bronze Age remains in the area, with two entrance portals and a recumbent altar-like stone. Like all the Cork and Kerry stone circles, it is remarkable for its beautiful site.

Return to Adrigole by crossing the **Healy Pass**, a simple but impressive feat of engineering which rises to a height of 334m (1,084ft), and takes in yet another panoramic view of Bantry Bay, before descending in a dramatic series of hairpin bends. From Adrigole retrace your steps to Glengarriff or Bantry.

This tour leaves the coast for a half-day drive through the Shehy Mountains, sparsely populated hills of west Cork. It is recommended in wet weather, as its attraction does not depend so much on panoramic views as the coastal drives. Cutting through the Pass of Keimaneigh, we visit St Finbar's island hermitage at Gougane Barra, a small lake surrounded by hills. From here the drive passes through small Irish-speaking villages beside a series of lakes to Macroom. The return route visits Béal na Bláth, where Michael Collins was assassinated, returning through the Cousane Gap, and the Maughanaclea Hills. *See map, page 40*

Take the N71 to Ballylickey, and the R584 **Kealkil** road which runs along beside the **Owvane River**. Take the left fork in Kealkil. About a mile beyond there is a sign for **Tedagh Candles**, a craft workshop where scented and brightly coloured, handmade candles can be bought directly from the maker. Another 8km (5 miles) on the same road is **Future Forests**, a nursery specialising in native trees which also sells interesting shrubs.

The **Pass of Keimaneigh**, or Deer's Pass, is indicated by a road sign. The road suddenly becomes narrow and the cliff-like sides get steeper as you enter into the pass. Many unusual ferns and alpine plants are found growing in the rock crevices.

Gougane Barra is just beyond the pass on the left, at the end of a 4km (2½ miles) track. The small, deep tarn, which is the source of the River Lee, is walled in on three sides by steep precipices which run with cataracts after heavy rain. The goat-like animals that inhabit the slopes are, in fact, mountain sheep. It is the sort of strange place that will inevitably have a myth belonging to it. In this case, the story features St Finbar, the founder and patron saint of Cork city, who killed a hideous dragon that he one day found lurking in the depths of the lake.

Fishermen at Cronin's

St Finbar's Oratory, a small stone-built chapel, can be reached by a causeway. The existing building is a 20th-century replica, built on the site where St Finbar supposedly lived and prayed before founding his monastery downstream in the place that is now Cork city. A pilgrimage to the chapel is still held on the first Sunday after St Finbar's feast day, 25 September. The courtyard, with eight cells surrounding an amazing coin-studded wooden cross, dates from the 18th century when another hermit priest lived on the island. There is certainly something special about the place, especially if you arrive early, before the majority of day-trippers get here.

The hotel, Cronin's, is where Robert Gibbings stayed in the mid-20th century when writing *Sweet Cork of Thee*, and it is still a

St Finbar's Oratory

friendly place with a great old-world air. A series of pleasant walks are laid out in the forest beyond the lake. Allow about an hour to make a circuit.

Return to the main road and turn left for **Ballingeary**. Like Gougane Barra, this is an Irish-speaking area. In the summer months, large numbers of Irish schoolchildren are billeted in these areas to improve their native language. If you are not picnicking, stop off at Ard na Laoi (inexpensive) for lunch, and you should hear Irish spoken all around you.

The **River Lee** widens into **Lough Allua** which can be seen on the right between Ballingeary and **Inchigeelagh**, another Irish-speaking village. Continue driving through **Kilbarry** on the R584, and note the strange, waterlogged landscape. This is **The Gearagh**, an ancient alluvial bog. Its Irish name means 'the wooded river', and it is actually a maze of tiny islands covered in dwarf oak. It forms a unique habitat for wildlife, including many species of birds and fish.

On reaching the N22, the main Cork-Killarney road, there are two options. Either turn left for a mile or so and take a look at **Macroom**, a small market town with a castellated stone gate dating from the 12th century in its main street, or continue on the main route directly by turning right.

After 10km (6 miles) on the N22 turn off at **Crookstown** and follow the signs for **Béal na Bláth** 4km (2½ miles) southwest on the R585. The monument consists of a large stone Celtic cross on a red brick dais and could hardly be uglier. It commemorates the spot where **Michael Collins** was ambushed and shot dead on 20 August 1922 during the Civil War. A memorial service is held here annually, and the road was widened to accommodate the crowds.

The R585 returns to Kealkil running for 55km (34 miles) across sheep-rearing hills known as the **Maughanaclea Hills** without passing through a single town or village. The **Cousane Gap** is less dramatic than Keighmaneigh, climbing gently from a hair-pin bend to a height of 232m (760ft).

At Ballylickey turn left for **Bantry**, right for **Glengarriff**.

Killarney & the Ring of Kerry

12. Killarney Basics

Killarney may be the most commercialised area in the southwest, but it is still possible to avoid the crowds and enjoy the great natural beauty of its lakes and hills at your own pace. The romantic scenery of boulder-strewn, heather-clad mountains, deep blue lakes dotted with wooded islands, and wild woodland has been preserved within a large national park. Be prepared to abandon the car and walk or hire a bike. You will soon discover why this area attracts so many people, many of whom come back for more. Allow at least one day. *See map, page 49*

Killarney has been a popular tourist destination since the days of the Grand Tour in the mid-18th century. Its scenery was considered on a par with the great Romantic landscapes of Switzerland and the Alps. Sir Walter Scott, William Thackeray and Queen Victoria were among many enthusiastic 19th-century visitors. With the arrival of the railway to Killarney in 1854, visitor numbers increased dramatically. Most of the myths and legends attached to Killarney's rocks and lakes were invented around this time to amuse the visitors, and are not to be taken seriously.

Follow the sign

Enjoying a visit to Killarney is largely a matter of attitude. You will not appreciate it from the inside of a car. You must get out into the air. As in the rest of Kerry, it is important not to be put off by rain. Any weather, good or bad, tends not to last more than half a day around here. In any case, the lakes of Killarney look especially good when seen through a light drizzle.

Remember that you are here for the scenery and the open air, not for the town or the shopping. Use the town to pick up maps and brochures from the Tourist Information Office (situated on

Beech Road beside the car park in the town centre), and to enjoy an evening meal in one of several good restaurants. Spend the rest of your time outdoors in the national park.

Try to arrive on the N71 Glengarriff-Kenmare road, especially if it's your first visit. This is a narrow mountain road that passes through a series of short rock tunnels between Glengarriff and Kenmare, where sheep graze in sparsely inhabited valleys. It approaches Killarney from a height of about 500m (1,600ft) through **Moll's Gap**, a corner that gives the first of many impressive views of the chain of lakes running through a rocky, partially wooded valley.

Stop about 5km (3 miles) further on at **Ladies' View**, where you will be looking south, straight down on to the Upper Lake, with the Lower Lake or Lough Leane beyond it and the Macgillycuddy's Reeks to your left. You will also encounter your first Killarney craft shop here, but you must turn your back on it to enjoy the view.

If you arrive in May, this road will be bordered by the large purple flowers of

Riding high

the rhododendron *ponticum*, an imported shrub which grows so vigorously that it threatens to overpower the native oak woods, and is being dug up in some areas to control its spread. In October and November, you will see the red fruits of the Mediterranean strawberry tree *(arbutus unedo)*. The play between the lushness of the mossy vegetation and the wildness of the mountains is a major feature of Killarney. Another great pleasure is the damp woodland aroma that permeates the mild Killarney air.

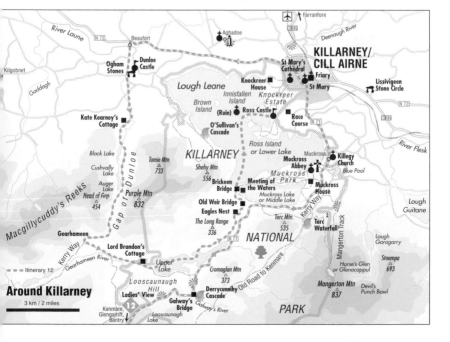

Refreshment at the entrance to the Gap of Dunloe

Rather than seeing Killarney as a series of sights to be ticked off a list, I would suggest doing one or two things in a leisurely way, and creating your own 'Killarney experience'. You may decide to stop on the N71 and climb the path beside the **Torc Waterfall**, following the second set of steps to the higher clearing and enjoying the view, which you can use to plan your next move.

A nice contrast to the wildness of Torc can be found in **Muckross Park**, a neatly trimmed lakeside area with signposted walks along gravel paths that forms the nucleus of the national park. This is a car-free zone, and it is a good place to take a ride on one of Killarney's famous jaunting cars – open horse-drawn carriages in which up to eight passengers sit in parallel lines looking out at the scenery.

The drivers, who are called jarveys, are traditionally great talkers, but whether you will hear about the myths and legends of Killarney or their own adventures on the building sites of London or Boston is down to the luck of the draw. Don't be surprised if you hear a phone ring during your quaint jaunting car ride; most drivers carry mobile phones these days in order to know where to collect their next fare.

Muckross House (September to June daily 9am–5.30pm; July and August daily 9am–7pm) was built in the 19th century in the Elizabethan style, and now houses a folklore and farming museum. You can admire the formal gardens without an entrance fee.

If you can spare the time, consider taking an organised half-day coach trip through the **Gap of Dunloe**, a narrow mountain pass formed by glacial action. The organised trip has the advantage of allowing you to travel through the gap on foot or horseback and back to town by boat without having to retrieve your car.

To reach the gap by car, drive 7km (4 miles) west of Killarney on the Killorglin

Ross Castle

road (N72) turning off at Beaufort. The gap itself is an unpaved path that stretches for 6.5km (4 miles) between the **Macgillicuddy's Reeks** and the **Purple Mountain**, which gets its name from the heather that covers it in the autumn. There is no motor traffic, but in summer there is a constant stream of ponies, jaunting cars and pedestrians going to and fro. The scenery hereabouts is first-rate, with a chain of five small lakes beside the road, and massive glacial boulders. But do not expect solitude. Most visitors turn back at the halfway point to return to their car, making it an outing of about an hour and a half.

The organised tour continues through the head of the gap down to the **Upper Lake** and goes on by boat. At this point it is traditional for the boatman to blow a bugle to demonstrate the echoes. The boat passes under **Brickeen Bridge** into the **Middle Lake**, landing at Ross Castle, a short walk from town.

Ross Castle (June to August daily 9am–6.30pm; September to May daily 10am–5pm) is a 14th-century castle keep that has recently been fully restored. You can hire a rowing boat here, and take a picnic over to **Innisfallen Island**, about 2km (1 mile) offshore. The wooded island has the remains of an abbey founded around AD600, which is famous for the *Annals of Innisfallen*, a chronicle of world and Irish history written in this remote and beautiful spot up to 1320 by a succession of monastic scribes.

Macgillicuddy's Reeks in the snow

A more serious walking option offers itself at the head of the Gap of Dunloe. The **Kerry Way** can be joined here, a 215-km (135-mile) circular walking route that goes around the Ring of Kerry. You can also pick it up in the Muckross Estate, and follow it along the Upper Lake, past Lord Brandon's Cottage, and into **Black Valley**, a continuation of the Gap of Dunloe carved by glacial action in the Ice Age, which offers precisely the isolation that you did not find in the gap itself. It is about 16km (10 miles) from Muckross into the Black Valley, and about 5km (3 miles) from the head of the gap. This section of the Kerry Way continues for 13km (8 miles) to **Glencar**, and passes near the base of **Carrantuohill** (1,039m/3,414ft), Ireland's highest mountain.

Returning by road from the Gap of Dunloe to Killarney, make a detour to **Aghadoe**, which is signposted 4km (2½ miles) outside town. The ruins of a round tower, a castle and a church built on a low hill date in part from the 7th century, evidence that the beauty of Killarney was appreciated long before the age of mass tourism. From Aghadoe there is a view back north along the lakes (the opposite direction from Ladies' View), which offers a memorable panorama, especially at dusk.

You can drive non-stop around the 190km (118 miles) of the Ring of Kerry in about 4 hours, but in order to see more than just the main road we have divided our tour into two shorter day trips. Besides admiring the scenery from the inside of your car, this also allows time to leave the vehicle, and visit some of the less-frequented side attractions.

Kenmare colours

The Ring of Kerry is justifiably famous for its combination of lush, subtropical vegetation and rugged seascapes. In July and August the narrow two-lane road can be clogged by a slow procession of tour buses and recreational vehicles. To minimise the effect of this traffic, we suggest taking the ring clockwise, starting in Kenmare, as nearly all organised tours go anti-clockwise. Another strategy is to start later than the tour buses, bearing in mind that these leave Killarney between 8.30am and 10.30am, and that the daylight lasts well into the evening on this western peninsula. If traffic and commercialism seriously bother you, do the Ring of Beara instead, or go straight to Dingle.

Leave Killarney on the N71 which climbs past Ladies' View and Moll's Gap before descending into **Kenmare**. This pretty market town is at the head of the long sea inlet known as Kenmare River. Unlike

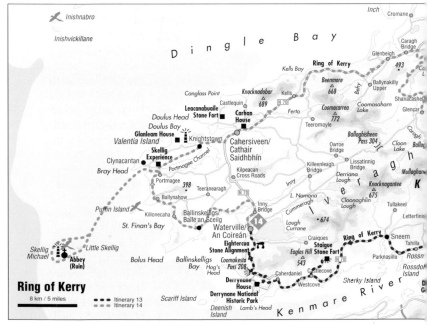

Staigue Fort

most Irish towns, which just grew, Kenmare was laid out in 1775 by the Marquess of Lansdowne in the form of an X. Tourism has brought new prosperity to Kenmare, which was always a popular base for anglers and golfers. Nowadays, it has two luxury hotel hideaways, several good restaurants and a selection of fashion and craft boutiques. The atmosphere is decidedly cosmopolitan, yet you may still come across a sheep market taking place in the town's wide streets.

Various themes of local interest are explored in the tiny **Kenmare Heritage Centre** (April to September Monday to Saturday 9.30am–5.30pm) which is located (along with the Tourist Information Office) in a pretty, green-gabled building in the town centre that was once the market house.

Join the N70 immediately to the north of Kenmare. Beyond Blackwater Bridge you will see lush, subtropical growth, evidence of the benign effect of the Gulf Stream. Wild rhododendrons, azaleas, camellias and bamboo are among the many plants that flourish on this sheltered south-facing shore.

Sneem is another pretty but untypical village, laid out English-style around a village green beneath a semi-circle of low mountains. A variety of indifferent modern sculpture is dotted around the village. Ignore this, and look for 'the pyramids' as they are called locally, beside the parish church. These small stone-built beehive huts inlaid with stained-glass panels appear to be ancient. In fact, they were built in 1990 with local labour, and designed by the Cork artist James Scanlon.

Castlecove is a small, friendly place 21km (13 miles) beyond Sneem with several good sandy beaches, and facil-

In Derrynane House

ities for deep-sea angling. A narrow lane beyond the church climbs 3km (2 miles) to **Staigue Fort**. This is a well-preserved example of a stone fortress dating from about 1500BC. It consists of a circular dry-stone wall, 35m (115ft) in diameter, varying in thickness from 4m (13ft) to 1.5m (5ft). A series of steps in the walls lead to a platform with good sea views. A donation is requested by the landowner. There is also an exhibition centre with audio-visual display (daily 10am–9pm) based at the Staigue Fort Hotel 3km (2 miles) from the fort itself.

Derrynane House (May to September Monday to Saturday 9am–6pm, Sunday 11am–7pm; April and October Tuesday to Sunday 1–5pm; November to March weekends only 1–5pm) is 2km (1 mile) beyond **Caherdaniel**. The house belonged to Daniel O'Connell (1775–1847), also known as The Liberator, who is remembered chiefly for his successful campaign for Catholic emancipation (granting civil rights to Catholics), a battle won in 1829.

O'Connell is still a great hero in this part of the world, and the house contains a greatly respected collection of his personal possessions and furniture. To some visitors the house may seem a little under-furnished, but at least the few bits and pieces on show really did belong to O'Connell. These range from a magnificent throne-like carved chair to the pistol with which O'Connell killed a man in a duel in 1815. The 130 hectares (320 acres) of woods surrounding the house have pleasant if unexciting walks, and access to an attractive sandy beach.

The next stretch of road which crosses Lamb's Head and winds along the edge of Ballinskelligs Bay has some of the best views on

Overlooking Derrynane Estate

the Ring, with vistas of rocky coastline backed by rugged green hills. **Waterville**, 15km (9 miles) northwest of Caherdaniel, is a popular base for golfers, who enjoy the famous links, and anglers, who have a choice of deep-sea fishing in Ballinskelligs Bay or angling on Lough Currane.

If you are based in Killarney, we suggest, in good weather only, returning via **Inny Bridge** on the relatively unfrequented road that runs up the middle of the Iveragh peninsula, turning right after 29km (18 miles) at Bealalaw Bridge to the Ballaghbeama Gap on the R588. This brings you to Moll's Gap, and gives you another chance to enjoy the best approach to Killarney in what will undoubtedly be a new and different light.

If remote pot-holed roads where you will encounter more sheep than people are not to your liking, then retrace your steps along the Ring through Kenmare, or alternatively stay overnight in the Waterville area.

14. The Ring of Kerry – Waterville to Killorglin

This is a leisurely day trip taking in the island of Valentia and the north coast of the Iveragh peninsula. There is a chance to take a boat to the rocky Skellig Islands, to look at the cliff-top monastery and watch the large colony of seabirds. Beyond Cahersiveen, there is magnificent coastal scenery. The quiet beauty found at Caragh Lake, a few minutes inland, provides a peaceful contrast. *See map, page 52*

Overlooking Ballinskelligs Bay

At Inny Bridge, just north of Waterville, turn left on the R567 for Ballinskelligs, an Irish-speaking area. Beyond the village the road travels through the glen, and offers the best views so far of the Skellig Islands – conical Skellig Michael, Little Skellig, and Puffin Island. The views get even better beyond the glen, as the road climbs the Coomanaspig Pass, revealing an impressive arc of coast and mountains.

At **Portmagee** the road crosses to Valentia Island on a causeway built in 1970. The name Valentia has nothing to do with Spain, but is from the Irish *Béal Innse*, the name of the channel dividing the island from the mainland. The island is 11km (7 miles) long and 3km (2 miles) broad, a quiet place with a population of about 700. The original transatlantic cable connecting Europe with Newfoundland was laid from here between 1857 and 1865.

The Skellig Experience (tel: 066-76306; April to June and September daily 9.30am–5pm; July and August to 7pm), on the Valentia side of the causeway, is an especially dull example of this new,

Buried on the Ring of Kerry

often rather fatuous species, the visitor centre. However, if the weather prevents you from visiting the real thing, it is better than nothing.

Skellig Michael (accessible May to September, weather permitting) was inhabited by monks from the 7th until the 12th century. It rises in a cone shape to a double peak 186m (610ft) and 217m (712ft) high. A flight of over 500 steps leads to the monastery, which is built of dry stone with no mortar. The monastery, which is sited on the edge of a dizzy precipice, consists of a group of beehive-shaped cells, two oratories and a pair of crosses, enclosed by a dry stone wall. Until early in the 20th century, Skellig Michael was a place of pilgrimage for penitents. It has recently undergone major restoration work to enable it to cope with increased visitor numbers. Resident wardens (student archaeologists) give a short talk in the monastery and ensure that this sacred and ecologically fragile site is treated with due respect. The boat trip is an exciting crossing, notorious for a heavy swell, even in fine weather. Landing on Skellig Michael cannot be guaranteed, due to the same swell, but if landing is unlikely, you will be warned. This trip may not be the most comfortable of your itinerary, but it may well be the most memorable. Allow a long half day, typically leaving Portmagee

Cahersiveen

at 10am, returning around 2.30pm. Landing on **Little Skellig** is prohibited as it is a bird sanctuary, the breeding ground of over 20,000 pairs of gannets. The boat circles close enough to make this an exciting outing for photographers.

Knightstown at the eastern tip of Valentia is a sleepy place, eerie in its quietness. Just outside Knightstown **Glanleam House** (June to October 11am–5pm, or by appointment, tel: 066-947 6176) is surrounded by subtropical gardens that sweep down to the sea.

Return to the mainland by car ferry from Knightstown and follow the R565 to **Cahersiveen** (pronounced Cah-her-sigh-*veen*). This is the chief market town for the Iveragh peninsula, but do not expect a buzzing metropolis. Many of its modest Victorian buildings are in need of renovation, and there is a strong feeling of a place that has seen better days.

The best thing in Cahersiveen is the community-funded visitor centre, **The Barracks** (mid-March to October Monday to Friday 10am–5pm [8pm August], Saturday 11am–5pm, Sunday 1–5pm; November to mid-March by appointment, tel: 066-947 2724). This is an exotic-looking, white-turreted building. The story goes that it should have been built in India, on the Northwest Frontier, but owing to a mail-room mix-up the plans were sent to Ireland instead. In fact, its architect, Enoch Trevor Owen, habitually built in what he called the Schloss style, and looked at from another angle, his design suits the hill-backed location very well. But why spoil a good story?

Originally built for police reinforcements after the 1867 Fenian uprising, this gorgeous white elephant was recently restored from a ruin – see the photographs of its former state inside – and houses an amusing and informative series of exhibitions on the Great Southern Railway, the 1916 Rising, the mid-19th-century Famine and other topics of local interest.

To improve your impression of Cahersiveen follow the sign outside The Barracks to the pier. The prettiest part of town is its backside, which overlooks the wide estuary of the River Ferta and the green hills beyond.

Part of the N70 beyond Cahersiveen runs along the **Gleensk Viaduct** which was built for the short-lived Great Southern and Western Railway. In certain weather conditions, the coast of the Dingle peninsula, across Dingle Bay, can appear uncannily close.

Glenbeigh is a popular touring base, convenient for both the sea and the hills. Head inland by turning right just north of Glenbeigh for **Caragh Lake**. This is a delightful, sheltered spot, popular with game anglers. The lakeshore is discreetly dotted with luxury hotels and holiday homes, mostly dating from the late 19th century. A scenic drive encircles the lake. By continuing to **Glencar** (a popular climbing and walking centre) and turning left, you will reach Killorglin without having to return to the coast and the Ring traffic.

Killorglin is a busy little village which makes the most of its position on the road between Killarney and Dingle. It is famous for Puck Fair, which takes place every year on the 10–12 August. On the first day, a mountain goat is crowned King Puck and installed on a tall throne overlooking the town until the evening of the third day. There are various explanations of its origin, but nowadays it is chiefly a drinking festival, and can get rowdy. Avoid Puck Fair if you value your peace and quiet.

From Killorglin, either return to Killarney on the R562, or follow the N70 north to Castlemaine and the Dingle peninsula.

Cahersiveens play ball

Dingle Peninsula

15. Dingle Peninsula South

This leisurely day-long tour heads west out along the Dingle peninsula. Since 2005, all signposts directing visitors to Irish-speaking areas must be in Irish only, so follow signs for An Daingean to reach Dingle. Beyond Dingle town/An Daingean, the scenery becomes truly spectacular in a wild, mountainous style. While it is possible to combine this tour and Tour 16, and return to Killarney the same day (a round trip of about 240km/150 miles), we suggest an overnight stay in Dingle to sample the traditional music in its pubs, and to enjoy some locally caught seafood. *See map, page 59*

−The weather can make or break a visit to Dingle. If the sea mist is down, consider postponing your trip until visibility improves.−

In **Castlemaine** take the R561, which gives good views of the coast of the Iveragh peninsula. **Inch** has 6km (4 miles) of sandy beach, backed by dunes protected by a long spit protruding into the harbour. On a fine day, it's hard to resist the temptation to stop for a walk and sample the clean Atlantic air.

Inch Beach

In **Annascaul** have a look at Dan Foley's Bar with its special paint effects; its flying gas bottle may be familiar from postcards. A magician by trade, and an expert on local folklore, Dan died in 1999 but his memory lives on. The South Pole (Bar) is also famous: it was the home of Antarctic explorer, Tom Crean, a local man, until his death in 1935. There is a pleasant 3-km (2-mile) walk to **Annascaul Lake** in the hills behind the village.

Dingle, the chief town of the peninsula, has a population of about 1,500, which can be doubled and trebled in the summer. Backed by mountains, Dingle faces on to a sheltered harbour. Until the 16th cen-

Dingle harbour

tury, it was a walled town, and the chief port of Kerry, and had regular trade with France and Spain. It is in an Irish-speaking area, as is all the peninsula west of Annascaul. The peninsula's Irish name is *Corca Dhuibhne* (pronounced Curkah-gwee-nee).

Dingle's popularity as a tourist destination increased dramatically after David Lean's filming nearby of *Ryan's Daughter* in 1969, and has been growing ever since. A further boost occurred in 1985 with the arrival from the wild of a friendly bottle-nosed dolphin known as Fungi, which will play for hours with swimmers (you'll need a wet suit), and follows boats in and out of the harbour. Weather permitting, you can find a boat at the pier to take you to see the dolphin.

Dingle has a good-sized fishing fleet. It offers an unusual and very appealing combination of the bucolic – farmers regularly come to town on their tractors, perhaps with a few sheep in the trailer behind – and the sophisticated, with a choice of serious restaurants and craft shops. The pier area is marred by a proliferation of postcard and souvenir shops. There is a triangular walk from the pier area, up Green Street, down Main Street and back along the Mall to the pier that takes you past the best shops, pubs and restaurants.

Continue west on the R559 through **Ventry**, a small village. At the western end of Ventry harbour, 6km (4 miles) beyond the town, **Dunbeg**, an Iron Age promontory fort, can be seen below the road. Its massive stone ramparts reach a thickness of almost 8m (24ft), and overhang the sea. It probably served as a refuge in times of danger,

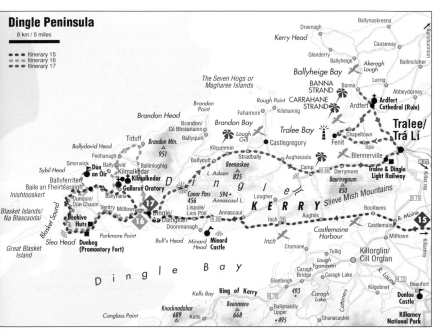

Dingle Peninsula

8 km / 5 miles

Island seal

and as a coastal defence. It is still used by sea birds, and you might spot seals basking in the sea below.

Between Ventry and Slea Head over 400 *clocháns* or 'beehive' huts have been found. The farmers have put up signs saying 'Prehistoric Beehive Huts', and may charge you a nominal sum to visit them. These small conical cells or huts of unmortared stone are not, in fact, prehistoric; the oldest date from the early Christian period, 5th–8th century, and were used by hermit monks. Others were built as recently as the 19th century to house farm implements. The area is still farmed by small-time sheep farmers, and it seems only right that the thousands of people crossing their lands should contribute a little something to their coffers. It may be a beautiful spot to visit, but it's a hard life out here for the farmer.

The road climbs westward around Eagle Mountain to **Slea Head**, and you will surely want to stop at one of the viewing points to take in the magnificent panorama. This is the view everyone expects when they imagine the west of Ireland – majestic tall grey cliffs, green fields, blue sea and sky meeting at a far horizon. If the sea and sky really are deep blue on your visit, you have indeed been blessed.

The group of seven rocky islands offshore are the **Blasket Islands**. The largest one, **The Great Blasket**, is about 7km (4 miles) long and 1.5km (¾ mile) wide. It was inhabited until 1953. The islanders were great story-tellers, and have made a lasting contribution to Irish literature. The best-known work is *The Islandman*, a memoir written in Irish in 1937 by Tomás Ó Crohan. You'll find no better book to read while visiting the area.

Louis Mulcahy's studio

Below Mount Eagle is the village of **Dunquin**, a scattered settlement whose harbour was once the landing point for the Blasket islanders. You may want to stop off at Dunquin Pier, where, weather permitting, you can walk down the steep, concrete path which follows the contours of the cliff face to a tiny landing place. The islanders landed here in curraghs, open fishing boats made of tarred animal hide stretched over wooden laths, examples of which can still be seen near the pier, resting on their stands like giant black beetles.

Boats go to the island regularly in the summer, weather permitting. It is a moving experience to walk the paths of the deserted island and visit the ruins in which, until comparatively recently, hard but simple lives were lived. The **Great Blasket Centre** (Easter to September daily 10am–6pm, until 7pm in July and August) is a labyrinthine interpretative centre, built on a grandiose scale – which is odd, as it commemorates people who led unusually simple lives. It contains photographs of the islanders and records of their way of life and their language.

To get a more contemporary flavour of Dunquin, an Irish-speaking area that attracts many writers and artists, drop in to the well-signposted Kruger's Pub. Ask here for directions to the *Ryan's Daughter* schoolhouse if you're interested.

On the road between Dunquin and Ballyferriter it is worth stopping at **Clogher Strand** to watch the Atlantic waves pounding the rocks. You might also like to visit the studio-workshop of Louis Mulcahy here, one of Ireland's leading ceramic artists.

The R559 returns to Dingle through Ballyferriter and Miltown.

16. Dingle Archaeology

This tour of the archaeological remains at the tip of the Dingle peninsula can be done in about half a day, but allow a full day if you intend to climb Mount Brandon on one of the ancient Pilgrim's Paths. *See map, page 59*

–Return to Ballyferriter, either on the short route signposted north from Miltown, or by making the circuit of Slea Head again.–

Ballyferriter is a popular holiday centre, adjacent to several good sandy beaches. Walkers can follow the route-marked Kerry Way from here to Dún an Óir via Sybil Head, returning to Ballyferriter by road (approximately 5km/3 miles round trip). You can also drive by following signposts on the Dunquin road for the Dún an Óir Hotel.

The road passes the ruins of **Castle Sybil**, which was built by the Anglo-Norman Ferriters in the 16th century on the site of an Iron Age promontory fort. The larger tower on Sybil Head was built in the early 19th century during fears of a Napoleonic invasion. The cliff here has a sheer drop of more than 200m (700ft).

The remains of **Dún an Óir**, Fort del Oro or the Golden Fort are on the edge of Smerwick harbour above a magnificent sandy beach. In 1580, over 600 Spanish, Italian and Irish soldiers took up arms against the forces of England's Queen Elizabeth I. The fort was bombarded, the Catholic allies surrendered after a three-day siege, and were then massacred. The intention was to discourage any future attempts at European invasions in support of Irish rebels.

Kilmalkedar church stone cross

The whole area from here to Brandon Mountain in the north-east is unusually rich in early Christian remains. Early settlements by hermit monks in the 5th and 6th centuries, attracted perhaps by the remoteness and the beauty of the area, were followed by more social, educational settlements in the 7th and 8th centuries.

Gallarus Oratory (well signposted in the area) is an extraordinary little building of unmortared 'dry' stone, probably dating from the 8th century. It is in the shape of an inverted boat, with a door at the west end and a window in the east wall. Due to its method of construction, with overlapping stones, it remains as dry and solid as it was on the day it was built. The interior measures 4½m by 3m (15ft by 10ft). The contrast, when viewed on a sunny day, between the dark, walled interior and the brightness outside is unforgettable.

The small road uphill from the oratory (turn left out of the car park, and left again) leads to the ruins of a fine 12th-century Hiberno-Romanesque church, **Kilmalkedar**. The stone head on the doorway supposedly represents the church's founder, an early Christian hermit monk. On each of the four corners are animal heads, and there are two more inside the east window. On Easter Sunday there is still a local pilgrimage to the church.

In early Christian times, **Mount Brandon** was an important place of pilgrimage, and certain routes to the summit became known as Pilgrim's Paths. Others are known as Saint's Roads. One of these, the grassy cobbled middle path starting from Kilmalkedar church, has now been route-marked, as part of the Dingle Way. Buy a good map locally before setting out if you intend taking this cross-country route which travels for about 12km (7½ miles) via Lough Gal to Cloghane on Brandon Bay.

The main tour returns to the coast road, and **Ballydavid**. The village is noted for its curragh-building industry, and is a good place to get a closer look at the local style of boat-building. At

Gallarus Oratory

Kilmalkedar Church

Brandon Creek, St Brendan the Navigator is said to have set sail on a voyage which led him across the Atlantic to America. The modern explorer Tim Severin gave added credibility to the story of St Brendan's travels in 1977, when he and his crew sailed from Brandon Creek to Newfoundland in a boat made in the traditional style from animal hides.

From Brandon Creek a section of the Kerry Way footpath runs along a clifftop and inland to climb Mount Brandon (915m/3,116ft). Also recommended is the ascent from Faha near Cloghane, accessible via the Conor Pass. This Saint's Road, or Pilgrim's Path is the most dramatic approach, following a valley created by glacial activity, with a string of lakes below it. Walkers should allocate about five hours for the round trip in both cases.

Return to Dingle.

17. North Kerry – Including Bad-weather Options

An alternative to weather-dependent scenic drives and walks, this day-long tour explores the weather-proof options available in Tralee, Kerry's chief town. These include a steam train and emigration museum with craft centre at Blennerville, a child-friendly, award-winning museum in the town centre, and the Aqua Dome water complex with its Sauna Dome to help you recover from the dampness of the Kerry climate. Then, on the possibly optimistic assumption that it will not rain all day, even in Kerry, we take off for Banna Strand, a flat sandy beach to the north of the city, passing through Ardfert with its 12th-century cathedral ruins. *See map, page 59*

It is possible to sit out one, or even two days of persistent bad weather in the bars and cafés of Dingle Town, but eventually even the most laid-back of travellers will be anxious to do something.

A trip to Tralee, by most standards a fairly ordinary town about 45 to 50 minutes away, will start to seem ever more attractive. Tralee also offers several ways of entertaining children, which may become a priority in bad weather.

Waiting for the rain to stop

There is no point in negotiating the Conor Pass in bad weather – take the N78 through Annascaul and Camp instead. However, if the weather is good enough to enjoy even a glimpse of the view, the **Conor Pass** to the north of Dingle Town should not be missed.

The drive is mildly hair-raising in all weathers (and positively terrifying in heavy mist) as you climb steeply to 456m (1,496ft) above sea level. In good weather, you can see all the way to the beaches of north Kerry on the other side of Tralee Bay (including Banna Strand where you are heading) from the viewing point at the top of the pass. Directly to the north is **Mount Brandon**, and to the south there are views over Dingle Bay. Going down from the top on the north side, the road winds along the base of great cliffs while the valley slope below it is strewn with large boulders. After about a mile, the road curves sharply over a deep gorge. Here, in a small corrie 30m (100ft) above the road, is Lough Doon.

There is a good long stretch of sandy beach at Camp, but not much else. **Blennerville**, outside Tralee town on the edge of Tralee Bay,

Geraldine Experience

was a major point of embarkation for emigrants to America during the famine years of the 1840s when the hinterland of Tralee was severely affected. Their experiences are recounted in a visitor centre beside the nicely restored windmill. The windmill dates from about 1800, and is the largest working windmill in Ireland and Great Britain.

A section of the narrow gauge **Tralee and Dingle Light Railway** (May to September daily 11am–5pm; tel: 066-712 1064), which ran from Dingle to Tralee before its closure in 1963, has been restored. A nostalgic half-hour steam journey can be taken from Blennerville into Tralee. Next to the steam rail's station on the western outskirts of Tralee (on the main road in from Dingle) is the **Aqua Dome**, a leisure complex of indoor pools and water slides, with a Sauna Dome for adults (April to September 10am–10pm; tel: 066-729150 off season).

Tralee is the county town of Kerry and its chief shopping centre (but don't expect much in this line). While it may seem like a booming metropolis after a few days in Dingle, Tralee is generally a quiet – one could say dull – place. The exception is the month of August, when Tralee's Race Week is followed by the Rose of Tralee Festival, an Irish beauty and personality pageant. Both events are accompanied by extensions to the usual licensing laws, and the whole town goes mad for a week.

The most attractive part of Tralee is the area near the museum, where there is usually plenty of pay and display parking. The nicely proportioned Georgian houses of Denny Street are mainly lawyers' offices. For lunch join the lawyers and other office workers in the Grand Hotel where you can eat informally in the Pikeman Bar or more formally in the dining room. The **Kerry the Kingdom Museum** (mid-March to October 10am–6pm; November and December noon–2.30pm) is at the other end of Denny Street in the middle of the pleasantly landscaped town park in a neo-classical building known as the **Ashe Memorial Hall**. In the base-

ment is a spacious Tourist Information Office. The museum is divided into two parts, and you can buy separate or combined tickets. Allow about 45 minutes each. The **Geraldine Experience** is a life-size reconstruction of market day in 14th-century Norman Tralee (complete with appropriate sound, lighting and odour effects) through which you travel in an electric railcar. It is perhaps best left to children.

In the rooms above the Geraldine Experience is **Kerry in Colour**, an enjoyable and informative look at the history of the county from the Stone Age right through to the present day. It uses relatively sophisticated audio-visual techniques, and also employs real people to impersonate historical characters. If you're lucky, you will encounter 'Sir Roger Casement', an Englishman who espoused the cause of Irish independence, and was caught trying to land arms on nearby Banna Strand *(see page 66)*.

Next door to the museum is the headquarters of **Siamsa Tíre**, the National Folk Theatre of Ireland. Performances feature song, dance and mime, and present an idealised version of life in rural Ireland of old (April to October; tel: 066-712 3055). Serious fans of traditional Irish music should contact Comhaltas Ceolteoiri Eireann, a national organisation that encourages traditional music, song and dance in an informal atmosphere, by ringing Crersa Feiritear on 066-915 6290. They don't hold shows of their own, but will tell you where to find the best traditional music locally.

The countryside to the north of Tralee is flatter and more sheltered than Dingle. Take the R558 which travels along the edge of **Tralee Bay** to Spa and **Fenit**, a small fishing port which is nowadays the harbour for Tralee. Even if the weather continues to hide the views, it is worth continuing to **Ardfert**. Ardfert is famous as the site of a monastery founded by St Brendan (AD483–578). It became an episcopal see in the 12th century.

The romantic ruins in red and grey stone are of a cathedral dating mainly from the 13th century which was in use until 1641. The

Walking while the tide rolls out

west door, with its rounded arches, is a good example of the Hiberno-Romanesque style, while the enormous triple window in the east gives an idea of the one-time scale of this church. There are the remains of two smaller churches in the grounds. In the grounds of the adjoining Ardfert Abbey (a substantial house which was burnt to the ground during the Civil War in 1921) are the ruins of a 15th-century Franciscan Friary.

A mile west of Ardfert is a signpost for **Casement's Fort**. This is a single-rampart earthen fort, renamed recently because it was here that the patriot Sir Roger Casement was arrested on Good Friday 1916 after landing at Banna Strand with arms for the Easter Rising. He was subsequently hanged in London for high treason on 3 August 1916. His body was returned to Ireland in 1965 to be interred with full military honours.

Controversy still persists about Casement's sexual orientation, with more and more evidence suggesting that he was homosexual. Irish Gay Rights campaigner Senator David Norris refers to Casement as 'the Great Irish Fairy', and there have been suggestions among the Irish gay community that Sir Roger should be canonised as the world's first gay saint.

About 2km (1¼ miles) beyond Ardfert is an access road to **Banna Strand** which leads to a network of unpaved roads connecting holiday homes to the beach via the dunes. Persevere among this maze and you will discover another monument to Sir Roger, commemorating his landing here from a German U-Boat. Banna Strand, a sandy beach backed by low dunes, is an atmospheric spot, great for walking in any weather, even if you cannot see the magnificent view across Tralee Bay to the mountains of Dingle.

The day over, return to Tralee on the R551. From Tralee the road runs north to **Listowel**, a market town lying in the flat north Kerry plain, and **Ballybunion**, a seaside resort famous for its golf links. It also offers traditional hot seaweed baths (May to mid-October; tel: 068-27469), the perfect antidote to rainy weather. The main N21 at Abbeyfeale continues to **Limerick** and **Shannon Airport**.

Ardfert Monastery

Shopping

While nobody could claim that the southwest is a shopper's paradise, few visitors leave without at least buying a hand-knitted sweater, a tweed cap or a ceramic puffin. You'll soon notice that many craft shops stock the same old lines. However, the better ones are full of attractive, well-designed goods, ranging from hand-woven scarves to hand-turned wooden salad bowls, linen shirts, uncut lead-crystal wine glasses and stylish rainwear.

Knitwear for sale in Sneem village

Many locals, myself included, regularly buy clothes and home furnishings from craft shops. They aren't there just to entice the visitors. But because craft shops are so numerous in the southwest, I have been highly selective in my recommendations, and have listed only those places that provide something a little bit different.

What to Buy

Cork city has an excellent department store, and an interesting 'left-bank' area. Blarney has the biggest craft shop in Ireland, while Kinsale has a relatively upmarket range of art galleries, craft and antique shops. There is a thriving tradition of ceramic-making in the area, with products ranging from pieces of original art to practical cookware. There are also several small galleries, selling original art at affordable prices.

The southwest is the place to treat yourself to a whole side of wild salmon, preferably smoked in one of the region's small smokehouses, like Ummera of Timoleague or Hederman's of Cobh. Whole cheeses also travel well. Milleens, Durrus and Gubbeen are all made on small farms in west Cork.

The shops recommended in the following pages are listed by town. As you will notice, the further west you go, the fewer shopping opportunities there are.

Kinsale

Boland's, Barry's Place, **Irish Arts & Crafts**, Main Street, **Stone Mad**, Newman's Mall, and the **Heather Mountain**, Market Street, are all design-conscious craft shops with a different range of goods. **Pat Dolan**, silversmith, and his son Dominic, Pearse Street, design and make jewellery. Watch lead crystal being cut by hand and purchase it at **Kinsale Crystal**, Market Street. **Keane on Ceramics**, Pier Road, displays goods by about 30 of Ireland's leading ceramic artists. There is a group of art galleries behind the town park on Main Street: **The Irish Print Shop** has a big choice of affordable works by contemporary artists; **Giles Norman** sells his own black and white photographs of the Irish countryside. **The Kinsale Art Gallery**, Pier Head, sells original work. On Market Quay, **Victoria Murphy** sells jewellery and small antiques. For edibles, including local cheeses, try **Quay Foods**, also on Market Quay. For home-cooked gourmet treats go to **Guillaume Le Quin** at **Bolands-Le Quin**, Pearse Street.

Cork City

The main shopping area is Patrick Street. The biggest department store is **Roches Stores**, and the most upmarket one is **Brown Thomas**, both on Patrick Street. Brown Thomas has a good range of Irish crystal, including Waterford, and a whole floor of designer fashions, about half of them Irish. Turn off Patrick Street at The Body Shop to explore Cork's **Huguenot Quarter**. This is a small pedestrianised area with a mildly Bohemian air. For retro clothing and young designers, go to **Hale Bopp**, in Paul Street. **O'Regan's Antiques**, Paul's Lane, is one of a line of interesting antiques shops. **Meadows & Byrne**, Academy Street, stocks a good range of Irish ceramic tableware, while **The Pine Pitch**, Emmet Place, sells restored country pine. Check out the **Vanguard Gallery**, Carey's Lane, **Form Gallery**, Paul Street Shopping Centre, and **Fenton Gallery** at Wandesford Quay off Washington Street for contemporary Irish art.

Cork – a great place to shop

Blarney

The original branch of the **Blarney Woollen Mills** is the biggest craft shop in Ireland. This vast warehouse, situated next door to Christy's Hotel, stocks everything Irish and more, including masses of Irish crystal, sweaters in all price ranges, high fashion, designer rainwear, Irish linen tea towels and other inexpensive souvenirs.

Clonakilty

Spiller's Lane Gallery (opposite the Catholic church and next to the post office) is a treasure trove of locally made pottery, paintings, jewellery, candles and other crafts. **The Tiny Studio** nearby at 9 Ashe Street sells ceramics, textiles and jewellery, hand-made by the artist-owners.

Baltimore

Beacon Designs at Reengaroga on the approach to the village sells knitwear in unfussy, contemporary designs. **Ishka** at New Road has a funkier line of knitted bags, hats and scarves, while down at the pier the **Sherkin Island Knitwear Co-Op** sells traditional knitwear using natural fibres.

Schull

Cotter's Yard, Main Street, designs and makes stylish ladies clothes in Irish linen. West Cork cheeses are available at the **Courtyard Delicatessen**, Main Street, who will introduce you to the cheese-makers if you want to buy directly from them.

Bantry

The Craft Shop, Glengarriff Road (www.craftshopbantry.com) stocks only Irish-made crafts, over half of which come from County Cork,

including hand-made knives by Bantry's own cutler, Rory Conner. There is a market (food, household goods and clothes) in the main square on Friday mornings.

Adrigole, Beara Peninsula

Adrigole Arts was voted one of the best craft shops in Ireland by the Craft Council. It's worth a visit just for its superb location between seashore and mountains.

Allihies, Beara Peninsula

Allihies has several resident artists, some of whom sell directly from the studio. Ask locally, or phone the **Beara Community Arts Group** on 027-70765.

Schull sweaters

Pottery possibility in Dingle

Macroom

Quinlan's Pottery, New Street, has a large range of hand-made tableware, most of it Irish, and a selection of jewellery and Irish crystal. There is an open-air market in the town square on Tuesday mornings.

Killarney

Avoca Handweavers, Moll's Gap, sells tweed clothing and mohair rugs in a wide range of colours. **Bricín**, 26 High Street, has a more interesting range than most Killarney craft shops. **Frank Lewis Gallery**, Bridewell Lane (near the General Post Office), sells original paintings and sculptures.

Kenmare

Cleo, located on Shelburne Street, sells its own quality designs of both classic and fashionable tweeds, linen and knitwear, chiefly for ladies. **Nostalgia**, Henry Street, stocks a good selection of antique lace and linen.

Cahersiveen

The Old Oratory (town centre, near O'Connell Church) is an art gallery and craft shop in a converted church. **The Antique Shop**, Old Road, is a well-established business selling objects dating from 1830–1950.

Dingle

The Weaver's Shop, Green Street, sells beautiful hand-woven scarves and wall hangings by Lisbeth Mulcahy. Her husband **Louis Mulcahy**, is one of Ireland's leading ceramic artists, and sells equally sophisticated work at his pottery studio and shop beyond Slea Head at Clogher Strand.

Eating Out

Twenty years ago, you could probably count the number of restaurants (as opposed to hotel dining rooms) in the southwest on the fingers of your two hands, and, of those, over half specialised in steaks. Things have changed for the better, with a wide choice of small, informal restaurants offering varied menus.

The new Irish cuisine makes the most of the excellent beef, lamb, pork, free-range chicken and duck, with Atlantic coast fish and

shellfish in summer, and game in the winter. Many of the region's chefs are influenced by both classical French cooking and nouvelle cuisine. San Francisco and the Pacific Rim have also had a significant input, with younger chefs freely mixing Oriental and European influences.

New twists on bread

The emphasis is still on hearty fare, with the more traditional places still serving large portions of meat and fish, and often at least two different kinds of potatoes. If there is one weak area, it is salads and vegetables. The exceptions are the few places that specialise in vegetarian or organic food.

If you're staying in bed and breakfast accommodation, your day will begin with a large meal of cereal and/or fruit, and a plate of fried egg, bacon, sausage and tomato.

The best value in the Inexpensive category is bar food, generally served at lunchtime and early evening. In restaurants in the Moderate price range, there is often a good-value 'early bird' three-course menu available until 7.30 or 8pm. Restaurants are busiest from 7.30–8.30pm. At weekends and in July and August it is essential to book, particularly at the expensive establishments. Even expensive restaurants are informal; only the grandest country-house hotels expect jacket and tie.

Prices are per person, including wine.
Expensive – Over €30
Moderate – €18–30
Inexpensive – under €18

Atlantic seafood is superb

Fresh veggies

Kinsale

THE BLUE HAVEN
Pearse Street, tel: 021-477 2209
www.bluehavenkinsale.com
This small town-centre hotel is famous for its seafood, including lobster mornay and sole on the bone. *Expensive.* Bar food also available. *Inexpensive*

CRACKPOTS
Cork Street, tel: 021-477 2847
www.crackpots.ie
An intimate restaurant with an imaginative menu featuring Mediterranean and Eastern influences. The handmade tableware is for sale. *Moderate*

THE WHITE HOUSE
Pearse Street, tel: 021-477 2125
www.whitehouse-kinsale.ie
Busy pub-restaurant renowned for traditional Irish dishes such as bacon and cabbage, fresh fish and delicious homemade desserts. *Inexpensive*

Cork

CAFE PARADISO
16 Lancaster Quay, Western Road, tel: 021-427 7939, www.cafeparadiso.ie
Owner-chef Dennis Cotter's extravagant vegetarian cuisine, using fresh produce, makes this a favourite destination – even among carnivores. *Expensive*

IVORY TOWER
Princes Street, tel: 021-427 4665
Chef Seamus O'Connell serves unusual combinations whose inspiration may be Mexican, Japanese or French, among others. If squid and fresh pasta with a tomato and basil sauce appeals, this is for you. *Moderate*

ISAAC'S
48 MacCurtain Street, tel: 021-450 3805
By far Cork's most lively eatery. An eclectic menu with influences from the East and the Mediterranean is served in a converted warehouse. *Inexpensive*

Cobh

JACOB'S LADDER
Water's Edge Hotel, tel: 021-481 5566
The minimalist decor of this restaurant is counterbalanced by panoramic views of Cork Harbour from its wall-length windows. An eclectic East-West 'fusion' menu features local seafood, meat, poultry and excellent salads. *Moderate*

Kinsale–Timoleague

CASINO HOUSE
Coolmain Bay, Kilbrittain, tel: 023-49944
Light, fresh cuisine from German-Yugoslav owner-chef served in an impeccably converted farmhouse between Kinsale and Timoleague. The lobster risotto is delicious. *Moderate*

OTTO'S CREATIVE CATERING
Dunworley, Butlerstown, tel: 023-40461
www.ottoscreativecatering.com
Food lover's cliff-top haven. All produce is from Otto and Hilde's own organic farm, or local organic producers, and is cooked with simple flair by the owner-chef. Book in advance. *Expensive*

Baltimore

CHEZ YOUEN
Tel: 028-20136
Jacob Youen has brought a little bit of Brittany to west Cork with his harbourside restaurant. Eat shellfish with your fingers, in homemade mayonnaise; follow with rack of lamb, and, for dessert, *tarte tatin. Moderate*

Set for tea

Castletownbere

NIKKI'S
Main Square, tel: 027-70625
This friendly, unpretentious town-centre restaurant two doors from Macarthy's Bar is renowned for generous portions of local seafood, lamb, and steaks. *Moderate*

Killarney

THE OLD PRESBYTERY
Cathedral Place, tel: 064-30555
www.oldpresbytery.com
Once a residence for clergy from the cathedral across the road, this is now a spacious, two-floor restaurant, with wooden floors, candle-lit tables and an imaginative menu of local meat and seafood. *Expensive*

GABY'S
17 High Street, tel: 064-32519
The cheerful, rustic-looking dining room of this restaurant *(pictured right)*, with tables spread with cheerful red and white checked tablecloths, is owned by its Belgian chef who specialises in classic seafood dishes. *Moderate*

PANIS ANGELICUS
15 New Street, tel: 064-39648
Home baking and excellent coffee are among the strengths of this stylish town-centre café, which also offers a light dinner menu from May to September. *Inexpensive*

Kenmare

THE LIME TREE
Shelbourne Street, tel: 064-41225
www.limetreerestaurant.com
This pretty old schoolhouse situated in the town centre, owned by the neighbouring grand hotel (The Park), has an unusual menu combining more traditional Irish cooking with trendy Californian influences. *Moderate*

Ballydehob

ANNIE'S
Main Street, tel: 028-37292
The dining-room at Annie's is so small that orders are actually taken in Levis' pub just across the road. Annie Barry's cheerful little establishment has become a west Cork institution, known for serving the freshest local produce made with the tastiest light sauces, and followed by the most irresistible desserts. *Moderate*

Schull

ADELE'S
Main Street, tel: 028-28459
Adele Connor provides irresistible home-baking during the day, including Cornish pasties, while her son, Simon, cooks a variety of tasty home-made pasta dishes in the evenings. *Inexpensive*

DURRUS
Blair's Cove, Durrus, tel: 027-61127
A converted stone courtyard with a heated terrace overlooking the garden, this French-owned restaurant is the perfect place to enjoy a romantic night out, fuelled perhaps by a rack of lamb from the wood-fired grill which flickers at the head of the dining room. *Inexpensive*

GOLEEN
Heron's Cove, tel: 028-35225
Goleen occupies a modern house overlooking a quiet sea inlet known for its herons. It specialises in fresh local seafood simply prepared, often with fresh herb sauces to enhance the delicate flavour. *Moderate*

PACKIE'S
Henry Street, tel: 064-41508
Talented owner-chef Maura Foley serves organic produce in a bustling, stone-walled bistro. Inspiration may be drawn from Irish, Californian or Mediterranean influences. Make sure you try the Irish cheese selection. *Moderate*

Sneem

THE BLUE BULL
South Square, tel: 064-45382
Traditional country bar with restaurant serving local seafood, lamb and steak in a low-beamed back room, as well as bar food. *Moderate*

Cahersiveen

QC'S SEAFOOD BAR AND RESTAURANT
3 Main Street, tel: 066-947 2244
This stylishly converted old building with a large open fireplace is now a busy restaurant with a Spanish influence, with both seafood and steaks cooked Basque-style over a charcoal grill. *Moderate*

Dingle/An Daingean

FENTON'S
Green Street, tel: 066-915 2172
The cottagey dining room has a relaxed, informal atmosphere enhanced by candlelight. Try the delicious cassoulet of mussels with garlic and cream. *Moderate*

OUT OF THE BLUE
Waterside, tel: 066-915 0811
This is not much more than a tin shed on the road by the pier, behind a wet fish shop and deli. But it serves leaping fresh fish and seafood, imaginatively prepared, and so tasty that you forget the minimalist surroundings. *Moderate*

THE CHART HOUSE
The Mall, tel: 066-915 2255
www.charthousedingle.com
A new cottage-like stone building on the harbour side is now a cosy, atmospheric restaurant with a sophisticated menu that mixes classic and contemporary cuisine. *Expensive*

THE FORGE
Holyground, tel: 066-915 1209
Cheap and cheerful fare, including superior burgers and pizzas, and freshly caught fish. Children's menu. *Inexpensive*

Tralee

RESTAURANT DAVID NORRIS
Ivy House, Ivy Terrace, tel: 066-718 5654
The owner-chef of this town-centre restaurant on the first floor of a modern building offers an imaginative menu in relaxing, intimate surroundings. *Moderate*

Colourful Gaby's in Killarney

Nightlife

Nightlife in the southwest centres around the pub. In Cork city, theatre lovers should check local papers, the *Examiner* or the *Echo*. Both the **Opera House** (Emmet Place, tel: 021-427 0022) and the **Everyman Palace** (MacCurtain Street, tel: 021-450 1673) schedule a mixture of serious drama, musicals and rock or folk concerts. In Tralee, the **Irish Folk Theatre**, Siamsa Tíre (Godfrey Place, tel: 066-712 3055), performs lively entertainment – dance, mime and music – to celebrate the rural past.

From June to September it should be possible to find live music played any night of the week. Outside these months, Friday to Sunday are the most likely nights. If the musicians are performing in the main bar, you seldom have to pay a cover charge. The exceptions to this rule are Killarney's 'singing pubs'. However, if a band is performing in a separate room with space for dancing, there'll be an entrance fee of anything from €4–15.

Music usually starts up after 9 or 9.30pm, continuing to closing time, which is midnight Monday to Thursday, 12.30am Friday, Saturday and Sunday. The exception is the spontaneous session, which can happen anytime. These usually consist of a group of friends or musical colleagues taking turns to do a solo: be prepared to join in if anyone in your group is at all musical. Failing that, if you have been enjoying the entertainment, it is the local custom to offer to buy a round of drinks for the performers. Total hush is not usually expected while music is being played, but use your own judgement. If everyone in the pub falls silent and stares at the

Enjoying a round

THE SPECKLED DOOR
Old Head Village, tel: 021-477 8243
There is no organised music at this friendly country pub, but there is a conservatory and beer garden overlooking the Atlantic, a pool table, and the occasional sing-song.

Cork

AN BODHRAN
42 Oliver Plunkett St, tel: 021-437 1392
A *bodhrán* is a hand-held drum, used in Irish traditional music sessions. These are a regular feature at this old-fashioned city-centre pub.

THE LONG VALLEY
Winthrop Street, tel: 021-427 2144
Old show tunes or marching songs blare out from an old gramophone in this Cork institution. Students, artists, poets and other eccentrics go there for its massive doorstep sandwiches, and stay for the chat.

THE LOBBY
Union Quay, tel: 021-431 1113
One of the city's leading music pubs. Free traditional sessions downstairs on Mondays, Tuesdays and Fridays, and a separate venue upstairs with an entrance charge for big name Irish and international folk artistes.

AN SPAILPIN FANACH
28 South Main Street,
Tel: 021-427 7949
Atmospheric old pub where Cork's traditional music crowd hangs out. Spontaneous sessions most nights.

THE HALF MOON
Club rear of Opera House,
Tel: 021-427 0022
A late-night live music nightclub operating from Wednesday to Saturday only, The Half Moon offers a wide range of music, including occasional jazz sessions.

floor while a solo is being sung, then you should do the same.

Should you want to go on partying after pub closing time, unless you are staying in a licensed hotel where guests can drink at all hours, the only option is to pay an entrance fee of about €8 to a disco. The music won't be live, but the main point of these establishments is their drinks licence which allows them to sell alcohol up until 2.30am. Most discos have a policy of only admitting those aged over 21 only, and in some cases over 25.

Kinsale

THE SHANAKEE
6 Market Street, tel: 021-477 4472
Recently stripped back to stone walls by new owners, this spacious high-ceilinged bar attracts a youngish crowd and has a selection of folk, rock and traditional musicians playing at weekends and some week nights.

THE SPANIARD INN
Scilly, tel: 021-477 2436
Once a simple fisherman's bar with a large open fire, this is now one of Ireland's most famous pubs. There is a traditional music session in the main bar every Wednesday night at about 10pm all year round, and live music most nights in summer.

MANGAN'S
Carey's Lane, tel: 021-427 5530
The leader among Cork's clubs is strictly for the young and hip. The city's clubbing scene is subject to rapid changes. Other city-centre hot spots at the time of writing include **Vibes**, Carey's Lane, **Side Tracks**, Oliver Plunkett Street, **The Comedy Club**, Coburg Street, and **Club FX**, Lynch's Street. Friday to Sunday are the big nights and the action starts after pub closing time.

Clonakilty
O'DONOVAN'S HOTEL
Pearse Street, tel: 023-33250
O'Donovan's has a regular bar, which is a nice, quiet spot, and a smaller more folksy one in an alley beside the main hotel building, called **An Teach Beag** (the little house), where they have lively traditional sessions on weekends all year round, and nightly from mid-June to September. There are also occasional story-telling evenings which are worth catching.

DE BARRAS
55 Pearse Street, tel: 023-33381
This is a genuine old world pub *(see picture)*. Decorated with real memorabilia, this is Clonakilty's number one music spot, and attracts musicians from near and far.

Glandore
P. CASEY
Tel: 028-33716
People tend to overlook this simple little bar, which is the highest in the village, and as yet unrenovated. You could be stepping back into the 1950s once you go through the door. It is one of those rare bars where you never know who you might bump into, nor what you might end up listening to in the way of spontaneous music and recitations.

A genuine old world pub

Leap
CONNOLLY'S OF LEAP
Main Street, tel: 028-33215
This is one of the region's big rock music pubs, where almost all new Cork bands play their first gigs. Heavy metal rules here; it probably helps if you're under 30.

Baltimore
BUSHE'S BAR
The Square, tel: 028-20125
Bushe's isn't known for staging organised entertainment, but it's a great spot for meeting interesting people from all corners of the world. The marine charts on the walls of the bar pinpoint local wrecks and are well worth studying.

Ballydehob
THE IRISH WHIP
Main Street, tel: 028-37191
A monument to the Irish wrestler Danno O'Mahony, the Whip has lively music sessions featuring Irish ballads at weekends.

Schull
THE BLACK SHEEP
Main Street, tel: 028-28022
This is Schull's chief music pub, but before paying it a visit bear in mind that west Cork is not a fruitful area for traditional music. What locals tend

to like is a ballad session where everyone sings along to old favourites.

Bantry

THE ANCHOR BAR
New Street, tel: 027-50012
Talk rather than music is the main activity at The Anchor, which is one of the last great pubs of character in the county, chiefly due to the unpredictable sense of humour of the landlord and his son.

Glengarriff

THE ECCLES HOTEL
Glengarriff Harbour, tel: 027-63003
On Sunday evenings, the Eccles holds country music-style ballad sessions in the bar. These are popular with locals as well as visitors.

Castletownbere

MACARTHY'S
Main Square, tel: 027-70014
This old pub-grocery, made famous by the late Pete McCarthy in his book *McCarthy's Bar*, supplies the local fishing fleet with food. It's not the place to go for music, but it's the best place to ask what's on in town tonight.

THE OLD BAKERY
West End, tel: 027-70790
By day this stripped pine converted bakery sells tasty home-made food, but on Saturday nights it is transformed into a venue for live music, usually in the folk-rock range and often featuring a jam session by local artists.

Eyeries

CAUSKEY'S BAR
Eyeries, tel: 027-74161
Causkey's holds an old-fashioned singsong every Sunday from about 9.30pm, but the real reason for visiting, on any day of the week, is to look at the amazing view of Coulagh Bay that can be had from its back window.

Kealkil

THE BROWN PUB
Tel: 027-66147
This is a genuine old-fashioned country pub with a friendly atmosphere and occasional weekend music sessions.

Killarney

GLENEAGLES HOTEL
Muckross Road, tel: 064-31870
The Gleneagles is Killarney's entertainment mecca. It has an enormous cabaret venue that hosts big-name international artists, as well as Irish acts aimed at first-time visitors. Elsewhere in the hotel is a singing bar and a late-night disco.

Enjoying the chat

THE DANNY MANN INN
Eviston Hotel, New Street
Tel: 064-31640
There is no charge here for traditional Irish music sessions which start nightly at 9pm in the summer, and on most weekends in the rest of the year.

THE LAURELS
Main Street, tel: 064-31149
Unlike 'real' Irish pubs, many of Killarney's singing pubs charge an entry fee and hire a professional to lead the singing. It's all a bit bogus, but can be surprisingly good fun depending on the crowd. Singing starts at about 9.15pm, but you should get here earlier as it can get very packed.

In Dick Mack's

BUCKLEY'S BAR
College Street, tel: 064-31037
There are free Irish entertainment sessions nightly from June to September and at weekends the rest of the year.

Kenmare

FOLEY'S SHAMROCK
Henry Street, tel: 064-41361
A friendly, family-run inn in the town centre with music most weekends.

Sneem

SNEEM TAVERN
Village centre, tel: 064-45130
Come here to enjoy traditional music every Friday and Saturday from 9.30pm. Also hosts occasional ballad sessions.

Waterville

INNY TAVERN
Tel: 066-947 4512
This large modern pub is not at all picturesque, but it does have a good friendly atmosphere and regular set dancing sessions (a kind of very fast barn dancing) to live traditional musicians every Friday and Saturday night, and from July to September also on Wednesdays.

Portmagee

THE BRIDGE BAR
Tel: 066-947 7108
They will give you a free lesson in Irish set dancing here *(see* Inny Tavern *above)* if you turn up on a Tuesday, which is the special night for local guest artistes. There are also regular weekend sessions, nightly in July and August.

Cahirsiveen

THE SHEBEEN BAR
The East End, tel: 066-947 2361
Live entertainment is provided on two nights a week off season and seven nights a week in July and August.

Glenbeigh

THE RED FOX INN
Tel: 066-976 9184
A large roadhouse with its own Bog Village Museum next door, The Red Fox lays on traditional entertainment from May to September.

Dingle

It is easy to find music in Dingle and district as almost every pub has very good music every night during summer. These three are a bit different; if you manage to visit all three in one evening, you can really claim to know the Dingle pub scene.

O'FLAHERTY'S
Bridge Street, tel: 066-915 1461
Dingle is renowned for traditional music, and this stone-floored bar is the most atmospheric in which to hear it. A session can start up at any time of the day, but the safest bet is after 10pm.

DICK MACK'S
Green Street, tel: 066-915 1960
Small and cramped, and unlikely to win any awards for snazzy decor, one half of this dusty old pub houses a somewhat neglected leather business, while the other half is host to numerous discerning visitors. Music may or may not happen at any time.

MAIRE DE BARRA
Strand Street, tel: 066-915 1215
Food is served here until 8.30pm, after which the music starts up. There are organised sessions nightly from June to September and at weekends all year round.

Calendar of Special Events

Details of these events and exact dates are available from **Cork Kerry Tourism**, Grand Parade, Cork, tel: 021-425 5100, www.corkkerry.ie.

JANUARY

The point-to-point season starts. Steeplechases are held in a different location in the Cork area every Sunday from about 2pm, until the end of May. Tel: 021-427 7655 for details.

FEBRUARY

The feast of **St Brigid** is on 2 February, and the **Biddy Festival** is a bilingual event in Waterville the following week celebrating her feast and the indigenous culture of south Kerry.

MARCH

St Patrick's Day, 17 March, is a national holiday, and is celebrated both on the day itself and on the nearest weekend. Cork city and many small towns have a St Patrick's Day parade, with pipe bands and floats.

APRIL

Tralee and Killarney are among the towns taking turns to host the **Pan Celtic Week**, a celebration of Celtic music, dance and song. There is a two-day race meeting in **Listowel** at the end of the month.

MAY

Heineken Sevens By the Sea is an international seven-a-side rugby tournament in Kinsale on the first weekend. On the second weekend, **Bantry Mussel Fair** celebrates Bantry Bay's mussel harvest. Baltimore's colourful wooden sailing boats hold a regatta on the last weekend that also showcases local seafood.

Resting up

JUNE

The first week is **Listowel Writers' Week**, one of Ireland's leading literary festivals. Mid-month in Blarney is the **Blarney Castle International Horse Trials**. The **Cork Midsummer Festival** features theatre, music, dance and other arts events. The last weekend in June marks the start of the

An Irish band plays on

racing, swimming races, greasy pole and Irish dancing competitions. In contrast, the **Rose of Tralee Festival** in the last week of August selects a young girl with Irish roots to be 'the Rose of Tralee'. The festival coincides with the **Tralee Races**.

West Cork Chamber Music Festival in Bantry House.

JULY

From mid-July until mid-August weekly concerts are held in the **Festival of Classical Music** at St Barrahane's Church, Castletownshend. The **Kinsale Arts Week** features readings, music, dance, and exhibitions mid-month. The **Killarney Racing Festival** attracts large crowds mid-month.

AUGUST

The Festival of the Sea in Castletownbere creates a two-week party in early August. The **Beara Arts Festival** held at the same time, celebrates the work of the area's many artists and craft makers, with exhibitions, practical courses and poetry readings. **Calves Week Regatta** in the first week of August is Schull's answer to the prestigious UK sailing event, Cowes Week. Leap and Glandore are *en fête* for the **Festival of the Carberies** in the first week, with street entertainment, pub singing competitions and sporting events. **Puck Fair** in the second week of August attracts a large crowd of merrymakers to Killorglin for a three-day party. Mid-month, **Allihies Races** combines horse racing and athletics in a festive day of traditional competitions. On the 15th Kenmare hosts a **Traditional Irish Fair and Festival**, the place to witness old-style 'horse-trading'. The **Glandore Regatta** on the third Sunday in August is a low-key event with yawl

SEPTEMBER

On the first weekend, the **Midleton Food and Drink Festival** showcases local produce – including Irish whiskey, while the **Cork Folk Festival** has an international line-up. **Storytellers** from all over the world gather on Cape Clear Island for a weekend in early September to swap tales. **Listowel Race Week** is held at the end of the month.

OCTOBER

The **Kinsale Festival of Fine Food and Fun** attracts bon viveurs to a unique three-day event on the first weekend of the month in which the town's restaurants showcase their collective talent. The **Cork Film Festival** in early October has a packed programme of screenings. The **Guinness Cork Jazz Festival** in the last week of the month is a massive event with an international cast of stars.

NOVEMBER

The **hunting season** starts, with meets every Tuesday and Saturday, and continues until April. The Irish **Rugby Football** season begins.

DECEMBER

The **Wren Boys**, disguised in traditional black face and straw masks, roam the countryside and entertain the towns on the 26th. Kerry is the best place for Wren Boys, but they are also seen all over Cork.

PRACTICAL information

GETTING THERE

By Air

Cork Airport (tel: 021-431 3131, www.cork-airport.com) handles flights from Europe, while transatlantic flights arrive at **Shannon Airport** (tel: 061-471444). **Kerry International Airport** at Farranfore (tel: 066-976 4644) has two daily Ryanair flights from London Stansted. Cork Airport is about 10 minutes outside Cork city. There is a regular bus service into the city centre. Shannon Airport is just west of Limerick, about two hours' driving time from Cork city. Farranfore is about half an hour from Killarney.

Ryanair (UK, tel: 0541-569569, www.ryanair.com) flies from London's Stansted Airport to Cork, Kerry, Knock and Shannon daily, while **Aer Lingus** (UK, tel: 0845-973 7747, www.aerlingus.ie) has direct flights to Cork from London Heathrow and ten other European destinations. Airlines providing flights between Ireland and the UK include **Bmi Baby** (UK, tel: 0870- 264 2229, www.bmibaby.com), **Aer Arann** (UK, tel: 0800-587 2324, www.aerarann.com), **British Airways** (UK, tel: 0845-773 3377, www.british-airways.com) and **Easyjet** (UK, tel: 0871-244 2366, www.easyjet.com).

By Sea

Swansea-Cork Ferries (UK tel: 01792-456116, www.swansea-cork.ie) operates a 10-hour car and passenger crossing between Swansea and Cork (mid-March to mid-November). It's cheaper to travel to Rosslare, either with **Irish Ferries** (tel:

Long and winding road

01-661 0511; UK tel: 0870-517 1717, www.irishferries.com) from Pembroke Dock or with **Stena Line** (tel: 053-33115, UK tel: 0990-707070, www.stenaline.co.uk) from Fishguard, each a four-hour crossing. **Irish Ferries** sails from Cherbourg and Roscoff to Rosslare. **Brittany Ferries** (tel: 021-378222, www.brittany-ferries.com) sails from Roscoff to Cork. Rosslare is about three hours' driving time from Cork city.

The cheapest way of all is to travel by coach. **Eurolines** (UK, tel: 01582-404511, www.eurolines.com) connects most major cities to Fishguard via Bristol travelling on to Cork, Killarney and Tralee: London to Cork is about 14 hours.

GETTING AROUND

By Car

All the itineraries in this guide require a car. Car hire is expensive and must be booked in advance. Ask about fly-drive deals.

In Ireland, as in the UK, people drive on the left, but both distances and speed limits are calculated in kilometres. The speed limit in towns and cities is 50kph (31mph), on regional roads (white R signs), it is 80kph (50mph), and on national roads (green N routes) it is 100kph (62mph). All occupants must wear seat

belts, and motorcyclists and their passengers must wear helmets. Traffic signs are the same as in the rest of Europe.

A good map is essential for travelling the highways and byways of the southwest. If you need more detail than is contained on the pull-out map in this book, I would recommend buying the 1:250,000 Ordnance Survey Holiday Ireland map of the South.

Irish signposting is a law unto itself. Those fingerposts that look so picturesque on postcards can in reality be twisted around and indicating totally the wrong direction. They are also very difficult to read in the dark. The older fingerposts give directions in miles; newer fingerposts and green road signs give distances in kilometres. It is not unusual to find both sets of signposts on the one route.

The national routes (N-routes) in the southwest are generally well maintained, two-lane roads with stretches of dual carriageway or 'slow lanes' to aid overtaking. Use these N-routes for getting quickly from one place to another, but do have a go at exploringe the smaller R-routes and even the unnamed roads, which often pass through the best scenery.

Drivers in the southwest are usually courteous and considerate, and hardly ever sound the horn except when celebrating a win at football or a wedding. However, they do tend to stop and block the road to talk to friends at short notice. There again, they are usually only too happy to wait for *you* if you wanted to block the road to chat to a passing friend.

Car Hire

Book well in advance, especially if travelling in July and August. Distances are not great in the southwest, and a small car is a good option.

Shannon Airport: Avis, tel: 061-471 094; Euro Dollar, tel: 061-472633; Hertz tel: 061-471369; Murray's Europcar, tel: 061-701200.

Cork Airport: Avis, tel: 021-428 1111; Budget, tel: 021-431 4000, Euro Dollar, tel: 021-434 4884; Hertz, tel: 021-496 5849; Murray's Europcar, tel: 021-491 7300.
Killarney: Avis, tel: 064-36655; Budget, tel: 064-34341; Murray's Europcar, tel: 064-30177; Randle, tel: 064-31237.

TRAVEL ESSENTIALS

The further west you go, the more limited the off-season choice of restaurants and accommodation. Many places in Dingle and the Ring of Kerry close down from October to Easter and the weather is pretty unpleasant from November to February. July and August are the peak months, when hotels and restaurants are busiest. Many visitors favour the 'shoulder season' – May/June and September/October when the weather is mild, and the roads and pubs are less crowded.

Visas and Passports

Passports are required by everyone visiting the Republic, except for British citizens. Visas are not required by EU citizens, Australians, New Zealanders or Americans.

Vaccinations and Health

No vaccinations are required. EU citizens require an European Health Insurance Card (EHIC) to receive free medical care in the event of a problem. Non-EU citizens are advised to take out health care insurance.

Customs

Duty-free allowances (not available to travellers between EU countries) are 200 cigarettes, 1 litre of spirits, 2 litres of wine, 50 grams of perfume and 250ml of eau de toilette. With regard to duty-paid goods, EU members can take in up to 110 litres of beer, 90 litres of wine and 800 cigarettes. Special rules govern the import of certain food products.

Weather

The southwest receives a lot of rain because the prevailing southwesterly winds bring fronts in from the Atlantic. On the other hand, the climate is mild, even in winter, becuase of the effects of the Gulf Stream. Severe frost is rare, and in certain coastal

Come rain and shine

areas unknown, as can be seen from the many subtropical plants.

Clothing

The southwest is predominantly casual in terms of clothing. Bring comfortable, preferably waterproof footwear. A strong, water-resistant leather shoe or boot is best and Wellington boots are extremely useful in winter. Ideally, clothing should be windproof and waterproof to handle the inevitable showers and the quickly changing weather that comes in from the Atlantic. Sweaters and cardigans are a must. Dining at all levels is casual but smart; gentlemen are expected to wear a jacket and tie after 6pm only in the smartest country house hotels.

Electricity

The standard electric current is 220 volts, 50 cycles. Most hotels have 110-volt shaver sockets. Wall sockets are generally three-pin flat, as in the UK.

Time Difference

Ireland observes Greenwich Mean Time and in accordance with daylight saving the clocks are put forward an hour in March and then put back an hour at the end of October.

GETTING ACQUAINTED

Geography

The southwest consists of the most southerly part of Ireland. Inland a broken chain of old red sandstone mountains crosses the region from east to west, interspersed with rich pasture land. At the coast, the land tapers off into five long, finger-like peninsulas. The coast is deeply fretted with rocky bays and sandy beaches, and warmed by the Gulf Stream.

MONEY MATTERS

The monetary unit is the euro. All prices are quoted in euros.

Foreign currencies can be freely changed throughout Ireland in banks and bureaux de change. Banking hours generally are Monday to Friday 10am–4pm, and to 5pm on one day a week. Automatic cash dispensers (ATMs) are found in all major towns and accept most major European cashcards and credit cards. UK currency is not generally accepted in shops and bars. Visa and MasterCard are the most widely accepted credit cards, and can be used in supermarkets, petrol stations, hotels and restaurants, while top hotels and restaurants usually also take American Express and Diner's Club.

Tipping

Tipping is not expected in bars, not even when bar food is served. In restaurants, it is the custom to tip at least 10 per cent of the bill.

Shopping for groceries

HOURS AND HOLIDAYS

Shops are generally open 9.30am–5.30pm. Supermarkets, petrol stations and small food shops stay open until 9pm or later. Late-night shopping in Cork city is on Fridays, when shops stay open until 9pm. In Killarney, opening hours are extended until about 10pm in the summer months.

Bars are open 10.30am–midnight Monday to Thursday, to 12.30am on Friday and Saturday, and noon–12.30am on Sunday. Some choose to open later than 10.30am: it is up to the landlord. All pubs are forbidden by law to open on Good Friday and Christmas Day.

Public holidays are:
1 January
17 March (St Patrick's Day)
Good Friday
Easter Monday
1st Monday in June
1st Monday in August
Last Monday in October
25–26 December

An inexpensive option

ACCOMMODATION

The price categories below refer to two people sharing a double room, B&B:

€€€€ Very Expensive: over €300
€€€ Expensive: €200–300
€€ Moderate: €120–200
€ Inexpensive: under €120

Book in advance between June and September. Reservations can be made at any Cork Kerry Tourism Tourist Information Office for a small fee to cover telephone costs, and a 10 percent deposit.

Accommodation in the region varies from top-grade country house hotels to simple farmhouse B&Bs.

Other Options

Guesthouses: Officially, any B&B with more than five bedrooms can register as a guesthouse. They are very like small hotels, but do not have a licensed bar or restaurant, apart from the breakfast room.

Bed & Breakfast: These can range from a simple room in a family home to rather grand country house establishments. Evening meals are often provided if notice is given before noon. Between June and September the better places get booked up very quickly, but you will nearly always be able to find a bed eventually. If the tourist office is closed, ask in the local pub if they know of a place.

The average rate for a double room en suite is €40 per person per night. Beds can be found from as little as €25 a night, to about €120 per person in the more upmarket country houses – excellent value when compared to the hotel equivalent. Most B&Bs will offer a reduction if you stay for more than one night.

There is a shortage of single rooms in the southwest. You have two options: book in advance and perhaps pay a premium, or travel off-season and hope to strike a deal on the night.

Hostels: These vary enormously in quality and standards of comfort. *An Oige*, the official Irish Youth Hostel Association (www.irelandyha.org), runs rather spartan establishments, often in very beautiful locations, which close during the daytime and enforce evening curfews. *Independent*

Holiday Hostels are recommended by Bord Fáilte. Go to www.hostels-ireland.com, or phone (tel: 01-836 4700) for a free guide.

Expect to pay around €12 for a dormitory bed, and €18–25 per person for a double room where available.

Self-catering: Cork Kerry Tourism (www.corkkerry.ie; *see Useful Addresses*) has a register of self-catering accommodation in the southwest, and publishes an illustrated guide every year. The average mid-season weekly rate for a two-bedroomed cottage is about €350, rising to €700 in July and August in prime areas. Some of the prettier cottages are in purpose-built 'holiday villages', so if you're expecting solitude on the side of the mountain, be sure that is what you're getting. **Country House Tours**, 71 Waterloo Road, Dublin 4, tel: 01-660 7975, fax: 01-668 6578, www.tourismresources.ie, specialises in renting out houses of character.

Cork

HAYFIELD MANOR
Perrott Avenue, College Road
Tel: 021-431 5600, fax: 021-431 6839,
www.hayfieldmanor.ie
This new luxury hotel is built in the country house style in a secluded setting 10 minutes' walk from the centre. €€€€

AMBASSADOR HOTEL
Military Hill, St. Lukes
Tel: 021-455 1996, fax: 021-455 1997
www.ambassadorhotel.ie
An imposing Victorian building has been

converted into a stylish, hill-top hotel with great views of the city and harbour. €€

CLARION HOTEL
Lapp's Quay
Tel: 021-490 8208, fax: 021-427 1489
www.clarionhotelcorkcity.com
A well-designed 200-bed hotel beside the River Lee in the centre. €€

HOTEL ISAAC'S
48 MacCurtain Street
Tel: 021-450 0011, fax: 021-450 6355
www.isaacs.ie
Boutique-style warehouse conversion in city centre, near bus and train stations. €€

ROCHESTOWN PARK HOTEL
Rochestown Road, Douglas
Tel: 021-489 2233, fax: 021-489 2178,
www.rochestownpark.com
In the southern suburbs, in its own woods. Award-winning leisure centre. €€

JURY'S CORK INN
Anderson's Quay
Tel: 021-427 6444, fax: 021-427 6144
www.jurys.com
This modern hotel charges per room, each of which can sleep three adults or two adults and two children. €

Rural idyll

East Cork

BALLYMALOE HOUSE
Shanagarry, Mildeton
Tel: 021-465 2531, fax: 021-465 2021,
www.ballymaloe.ie
Leading country house hotel. Characterful and impeccably decorated. €€€

BALLYMAKEIGH HOUSE
Killeagh
Tel: 024-95184, fax: 024-95370

www.ballymakeighhouse.com
Margaret Browne's picture-book-pretty farmhouse B&B has scooped numerous awards. Dinner by arrangement. €

Kinsale

THE BLUE HAVEN
Pearse Street
Tel: 021-477 2209, fax: 021-477 4268
www.bluehavenkinsale.com
Small, tastefully decorated town house hotel famous for its seafood restaurant. €€€

FRIAR'S LODGE
Friar Street
Tel: 021-477 3445, fax: 021-477 4363
www.friars-lodge.com
Sumptuously converted Georgian town house with excellent value rooms. €

GLEBE HOUSE
Ballinadee
Tel: 021-477 8294, fax: 021-477 8456
18th-century rectory in a quiet village on the River Bandon. Dinner by arrangement. €

Clonakilty

LODGE AND SPA AT INCHYDONEY ISLAND
Tel: 023-33143, fax: 023-33250
www.inchydoneyisland.com
A large hotel situated between two long sandy beaches; luxurious accommodation and leisure centre with seaweed and salt-water beauty treatments. €€€€

Castletownshend

THE CASTLE
Tel: 028-36100, fax: 028-36166
www.castle-townshend.com
An 18th-century house built by the ruins of a castle on the water's edge in one of west Cork's prettiest villages. €€

Glandore

KILFINNAN FARM
Tel: 028-33233 (no fax)
www.kilfinnanfarm.com
Simple accommodation on a working farm overlooking the harbour. €

Skibbereen

WEST CORK HOTEL
Tel: 028-21277, fax: 028-22333
www.westcorkhotel.com

Well run family hotel. The dining room is renowned for generous portions of fresh local produce. €€

Baltimore

ROLF'S HOLIDAY HOSTEL
Tel and fax: 028-20289
www.rolfsholidays.com
An old farmhouse and stone-built yard with good sea views and its own restaurant, this is more like a pension than a hostel. €

Bantry

BANTRY HOUSE
Tel: 027-50047, fax: 027-50795
www.bantryhouse.ie
One wing of this magnificent mansion over-looking Bantry Bay has been converted to an up-market bed and breakfast. €€

Ballylickey

SEAVIEW HOUSE HOTEL
Tel: 027-50073, fax: 027-51555
www.seaviewhousehotel.com
Comfortable, friendly and attractively decorated in the country house style. Extensive grounds overlooking Bantry Bay. €€€

Beara Peninsula

RODEEN
Castletownbere
Tel: 027-70158
www.welcome.to/Rodeen
Comfortable modern house on an elevated site overlooking the bay; surrounded by a subtropical garden. €

DZOGCHEN BEARA RETREAT CENTRE
Tel: 027-73032, fax: 027-73177
www.dzogchenbeara.org
An old farmhouse in the grounds of the Dzogchen Buddhist Holiday and Retreat Centre. Their cliff-top meditation room has to be seen to be believed; self-catering accommodation is also available. €

Killarney

CAHERNANE HOTEL
Muckross Road
Tel: 064-31895, fax: 064-34340
www.cahernane.com
A lovely old manor house in a secluded lakeside location. There is more sense of history here than at Killarney's other lux-ury hotels, even though most of the bed-rooms are in a modern wing. €€€€

CASTLEROSSE HOTEL
Beaufort Road
Tel: 064-31144, fax: 064-31031
www.castlerossekillarney.com
Situated near the Killarney Golf and Fishing Club. The grounds of this mod-ern hotel run down to Lough Leane. €€€

ARBUTUS HOTEL
College Street
Tel: 064-31037, fax: 064-34033
www.arbutuskillarney.com
This is a pleasant, Victorian, family-run, town-centre hotel with open turf fires and traditional music in the lively bar. €€

BEAUFORT HOUSE
Killarney
Tel and fax: 064-44764
This Georgian house in 16 hectares (40 acres) of woodland is a family home offer-ing B&B and self-catering cottages. Trout and salmon fishing in the grounds, and din-ner by arrangement. Dog lovers only. €€

KILLEEN HOUSE
Aghadoe
Tel: 064-31711, fax: 064-31811
www.killeenhousehotel.com
This red-gabled house was once a rectory and is now a small family-run hotel. €€

Ring of Kerry

CARAGH LODGE
Caragh Lake
Tel: 066-976 9115, fax: 066-976 9316
www.caraghlodge.com
A quietly luxurious Victorian fishing lodge offering trout fishing and amazingly peace-ful surroundings. €€€

PARK HOTEL
Kenmare
Tel: 064-41200, fax: 064-41402
www.parkkenmare.com

Derrynane Hotel

Victorian mansion set in extensive grounds sweeping down to the bay. A leading country house hotel with a deluxe spa. €€€€

BLACKSTONE HOUSE
Glencar
Tel and fax: 066-976 0164
At the foot of Carrantuohill in the wooded area between Killarney and Killorgan: an excellent base for walkers. €€€

DERRYNANE HOTEL
Caherdaniel
Tel: 066-947 5136, fax: 066-947 5160
www.derrynane.com
Modern hotel at the water's edge in one of the most scenic spots on the Ring. €€

SEA SHORE FARM
Tubrid, Kenmare
Tel and fax: 064-41270
www.seashorehouse.net
Substantial farmhouse in a peaceful waterside setting 1.5km (1 mile) outside the town. The land extends to the water edge. €

TAHILLA COVE COUNTRY HOUSE
near Sneem
Tel: 064-45204, fax: 064-45104
www.tahillacove.com
Modern, family-run hotel on a sheltered shore with its own gardens and pier. €€

ISKEROON
Bunavalla, Caherdaniel
Tel and fax: 066-947 5119
www.iskeroon.com
A small B&B in an idyllic setting overlooking Derrynane harbour with semi-tropical garden and private pier. €

Dingle

DINGLE SKELLIG
Tel: 066-915 0200, fax: 066-915 1501
www.dingleskellig.com
A lively, well designed modern hotel on the water's edge with leisure centre. €€€

GREENMOUNT HOUSE
Upper John Street
Tel: 066-915 1414, fax: 066-915 1974
www.greenmount-house.com
Award-winning modern guest house five minutes' walk from the town centre. €

HEATON'S
The Wood
Tel: 066-915 2288, fax: 066-915 2324
www.heatonsdingle.com
Just outside town on the road to Slea Head, this friendly modern guesthouse has won awards for its breakfasts. €

HEALTH AND EMERGENCIES

For any of the emergency services (police, fire or ambulance) dial **999**.

If you need medical or dental services, consult your hotel first: staff will recommend or call out a local doctor or dentist.

Visitors from the EU receive free medical services provided they have an European Health Insurance Card (EHIC); other visitors should take out insurance.

Guaranteed delivery

COMMUNICATIONS AND NEWS

Post

Postage stamps can be bought at all post offices and many craft shops.

Telephone

Public telephones are plentiful, but over half of them are card phones, so buy a card on arrival (widely available from newsagents and supermarkets). The minimum charge for a local call is 20p. Cheap rate applies from 6pm–8am and all day Saturday, Sunday and public holidays.

Media

RTE televison offers three channels, RTE1, RTE2 and TG4 which broadcasts in Irish. The British TV networks of BBC1, BBC2, HTV and Channel 4 are available by cable in the Cork city and harbour area, including Kinsale. Where reception is limited to RTE1 and 2, most hotels provide a choice of satellite channels in English and various European languages.

Cork city's daily newspaper, the *Irish Examiner*, has the best local entertainment guide for both Cork and Kerry. UK newspapers are widely available in the larger cities, though in the more remote parts of Kerry they still arrive one day late, and may have to be ordered in advance. (Hence the true story of the Kerry newsagent saying 'I can sell you yesterday's paper, but if you want today's paper you must come back tomorrow.') Many newsagents also sell *USA Today*, the *New York Herald Tribune* and, in the summer months, the leading European newspapers are widely available in the major tourist centres.

The official first language is Gaelic

LANGUAGE

These days, all Irish people can speak English, but most people living in the *Gaeltacht* or Irish-speaking areas prefer to live through Ireland's official first language. Gaelic, or Irish as it is usually called today, is a Celtic language related to Breton, Cornish and Welsh, but closer to Manx and Scots Gaelic. It was the language of the majority until the mid-19th century. When English took over as the language of commerce, the more prosperous Irish began to use it and Gaelic became associated with poverty and social disadvantage: the remaining Irish speakers were chiefly among the rural poor, the sector that was decimated by the Great Famine of 1846–48 and the subsequent mass emigration.

Irish survived in small, relatively remote regions, and is still spoken today in various pockets of Ireland, including the inland, hilly regions of west Cork, Cape Clear Island and the tip of the Dingle peninsula. It is still a compulsory subject in all Irish schools, and about 30 percent of the population claim to be Irish-speaking. Irish-speakers who have to live outside the *Gaeltacht* areas often choose to spend their holidays in Dingle or west Cork to exercise their language skills and absorb the unique culture of these regions, which is chiefly musical and literary.

ACTIVITIES

Angling

The southwest has a wide choice of lakes and trout and salmon rivers. For details of locations for coarse and game fishing contact the local Tourist Information Office or the **South Western Regional Fisheries Board**, 1 Neville Terrace, Macroom, County Cork, tel: 026-41221. Most seaports have facilities for deep-sea angling; enquire locally.

Cookery

The Ballymaloe Cookery School, Shanagarry, County Cork, tel: 021-464 6785, www.cookingisfun.ie, runs residential courses at all levels and specialised weekend courses with television cook Darina Allen and/or visiting celebrity chefs.

Cycling

Bicycles are widely available for hire in the southwest by the day or by the week. Bring your own wet-weather gear. **Irish Cycling Safaris**, tel: 01-260 0749, www.cyclingsafaris.com, organise 7- or 14-day cycling tours of west Cork with B&B accommodation and provides bikes, mechanical back-up, luggage transfer and details of cycling routes.

Horse Riding

Organised hacks last from one hour to three hours. Most places will lend you a hat and, if necessary, boots. Ask at the Tourist Information Office for the nearest stable. Places that advertise trekking generally cater for beginners as well as more advanced riders.

El Rancho Farmhouse & Riding Stables, Ballyard, Tralee, County Kerry, tel & fax: 066-21840, offers three-day and one-week residential riding holidays on the Dingle peninsula. For other options see the **Equestrian Holidays Ireland** website (www.ehi.ie).

Golf

It is advisable to book a tee time in advance at the more famous courses. There are many other places where you can usually just turn up and play – outside the busy months of July and August. Golf clubs and golf buggies are not generally available for hire.

Walking

There are three long-distance walking routes in the area: the Dingle Way, the Kerry Way and the Beara Way. Maps and leaflets describing the routes are available from the main Tourist Information Offices. Walking holidays in small groups are offered by **Walking Tours in Ireland** (tel: 066-976 2094; www.walking-tours-in-ireland.com).

Watersports

Glenans Irish Sailing Club, 28 Merrion Square, Dublin 2, tel: 01-661 1481, www.glenans-ireland.com, has a residential sailing school in Castletownbere. **The Oysterhaven Holiday Centre**, Oysterhaven, near Kinsale, County Cork, tel: 021-477 0738, www.oysterhaven.com, rents out sailboard equipment, including wet suits, and organises residential activity holidays. The **Castlepark Marina Centre**, Kinsale,

Horse power

tel: 021-477 4959 has scuba diving facilities. **Seafari**, Kenmare Pier, County Kerry, tel: 064-83171, is a marine activity centre which offers sailboarding, canoeing and waterskiing.

USEFUL ADDRESSES

Bord Fáilte and Cork-Kerry Tourism provide a free information service and sell a variety of tourist literature. For a small fee they will also book accommodation. The following offices are open all year weekdays 9am–6pm and Saturday 9am–1pm: Grand Parade, **Cork City**, County Cork, tel: 021-427 3251, fax: 021-427 3504, www.corkkerry.ie; Beech Road, **Killarney**, County Kerry, tel: 064-31633, fax: 064-34506; North Street, **Skibbereen**, County Cork, tel: 028-21766, fax: 028-21353; Ashe Memorial Hall, Denny Street, **Tralee**, tel: 066-712 1288, fax: 066-712 1700, www.shannon-dev.ie.

Seasonal offices are open from mid-May to September in the following towns: County Cork: **Bantry**, tel: 027-50229, **Clonakilty**, tel: 023-33226, **Kinsale**, tel: 021-477 2234, **Youghal**, tel: 024-92390. County Kerry: **Dingle**, tel: 066-915 1188, **Kenmare**, 064-41233.

FURTHER READING

Insight Guide: Ireland. Apa Publications.
Insight Guide: Dublin. Apa Publications.
Insight Pocket Guide: Ireland. With pull-out map. Apa Publications.
Insight Compact Guide: Ireland and *Insight Compact Guide: West of Ireland.* Apa Publications.
The Last September, Elizabeth Bowen. Penguin.
The Cork Anthology, Ed. Sean Dunne. Cork University Press.
Ireland 1912–1985, J.J. Lee. Cambridge University Press.
The Bridgestone Irish Food Guide, John and Sally McKenna. Estragon Press.
The Course of Irish History, T.W. Moody and F.X. Martin. Mercier Books.
The Islandman, Tomás Ó Crohan. Oxford University Press.
Mr & Mrs Hall's Tour of 1840, Ed. Michael Scott. Sphere Books.

ACKNOWLEDGMENTS

Photography	Geray Sweeney *and*
16T, 51, 56T	Carlotta Junger
5, 7T, 3T, 48, 60T, 81, 82, 92,	Marcus Wilson Smith
24	Alamy
23	Axiom
Back cover photograph	Marcus Wilson Smith
Front cover photograph	Alamy
Handwriting	V Barl
Cover Design	Tanvir Virdee
Cartography	Berndtson & Berndtson